The Sea Enchantress

PRAWNOGRAPHY

VICTOR GORDON

BLOOMSBURY

First published in Great Britain 1989
This paperback edition published 1990

Bloomsbury Publishing Limited, 2 Soho Square, London W1V 5DE

A CIP catalogue record for this book
is available from the British Library

ISBN 0-7475-0628-0

10 9 8 7 6 5 4 3 2 1

Illustrations by Michaela Stewart

Typeset by Rapid Communications Ltd, London WC1

Printed by Clays Ltd, St Ives plc

Contents

Acknowledgements

Recipe plagiarism has flourished since the second cookery book, and this one cannot claim to be a complete exception. A few of the dishes are original; most are in the public domain somewhere in the world. The rule I have tried to follow is to acknowledge in the text any recipe which I feel belongs, in some sense, to a particular author. Cookery writers to whom I have resorted most in my desktop and stovetop research are Alan Davidson, George Lassalle, Premila Lal, Maria Lambert Ortiz, Charmaine Solomon and, inevitably, Elizabeth David. To all of these I express grateful admiration.

Every section of the prawn industry which I have approached has been most helpful – without knowing for sure whether I was friend or foe. In particular, I thank David Sheepshanks, founder of Starfish Ltd, who encouraged this venture from the start, and his associates in Reykjavik, Ingi Konradsson and Heimir Fjelsted of Marfang Ltd. Through Marfang's kind offices I met Larus Aegir Gudmundsson of Raekjuvinsslan Ltd and Gunnar-Thor Gunnarsson of the good trawler *Audbjorg*, who showed me the sharp end – or rostrum? – of the industry: Gunnar-Thor at sea, Larus at the freezing plant in Skagastrond.

Half a world away I was initiated with equal courtesy, patience and openness into shrimp culture in Ecuador. To José Luis Romo-Rosales of Amazonas C.A., Antonio Pino Gomez-Lince of Promarisco S.A., and Angel Guevara of CIPAC Ltda – *muchas gracias*.

In North America, Greg Morton of the Bridge Street Café, South Dartmouth, Massachusetts was equally helpful about the cooking of New England – and New Orleans.

Finally, all thanks and love to my prawn-sated family – to Emma for tracking down rare species of prawn and prawnmonger, to Toby for constructive unstinted criticism, to Rupert for his Iberian expertise and to Juliet for enduring so much wholly undeserved – prawnography.

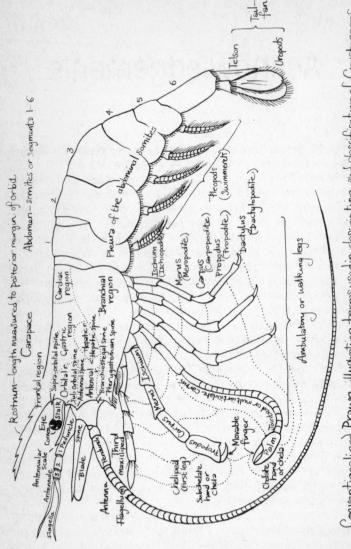

Conventionalized Prawn, illustrating terms used in description and classification of Crustaceans.

Introduction

Prawns are enchantresses of the sea – affordable luxuries which are voluptuously versatile in the kitchen, yet remain an abiding joy in their simplest forms. They complement the plainest cooking and compliment the most beloved – or difficult – guest. Prawns lure fishermen to the farthest oceans and ascetics to self-forbidden delights; they entice the greedy, the fastidious and the omnivore alike. When the celebrating Briton orders his prawn cocktail, he is expressing a timeless longing and a global instinct – while part of him, perhaps, yearns for the womb of life itself, the sea.

This book is a celebration of the prawn family and a guide to greater enjoyment of the world's favourite seafood.

What is a Prawn?

Within the class of crustacea, which also includes crabs, barnacles and sandhoppers, prawns and shrimps comprise the sub-order of *Decapoda natantia*, the ten-legged swimmers. Ten-legged, too, are the crabs, but they do not swim, they crawl, and so are called *Decapoda reptantia*.

There are hundreds of different species of prawns, most of them too small for human consumption, too rare, or too hard to extract from their deep-sea retreats. However, some 340 species are reckoned by the Food and Agriculture Organisation to have commercial potential, and well over fifty species are bought and sold on a regular basis somewhere in the world.

All these species have in common two pairs of antennae (as opposed to insects, which only have one pair), horn-like shells and five pairs of legs, of which the first two – in one species the first three – have pincers. They all swim by means of paddle-like pleopods located under their six-segmented tails or abdomens.

Edible *Decapoda natantia* range in length from under one inch to over one foot. The smallest, those up to, say, three inches long, are called shrimps in England and most Commonwealth countries. The true shrimp, *Crangon crangon*, goes brown when cooked, but the little pink *Palaemon serratus* is invariably called shrimp too, and is nowadays the more popular with the general public (which is perhaps a pity because they are less tasty). In the United States, all *Decapoda natantia* tend to be called shrimp whatever their size, though the term prawn is understood, and is still used in certain places. In this book, British practice is used except for recipes and references specifically connected with America.

For culinary purposes, prawns can be divided into three categories – small (shrimps), medium and large. This is puerile taxonomy but practical gastronomy. Practical in the first case because shops and markets seldom offer more than half a dozen species and often only one, two or three; practical in the second place because the differences in taste and texture, if not negligible, are seldom significant. For example, a dish which is delicious made with *Penaeus kerathurus* will work very well with any other large prawn. A partial exception to this rule is that small-to-medium warm-water prawns, large numbers of which come deep-frozen or dried to Britain from the East, are generally considered inferior to cold-water prawns of similar size from the North Atlantic. There is a theory that warm-water prawns are inherently inferior to cold-water ones because their faster growth leads to flabbier texture. However, many of the best prawns (*Penaeus monodon, Penaeus kerathurus, Penaeus vannamei*) come from warm or fairly warm waters. It seems more likely that hazards in the processing chain – long journeys to the freezing plant through tropical heat, relatively primitive process technology, inadequate enforcement of hygiene standards, even the quality of the water used – are the main reasons why warm-water prawns have done badly in blind tests.

There is a very important group of decapods which were at one time classified among the swimmers, but are now recognised as crawlers. The lobster, crawfish, crayfish and scampo are, it seems, elongated crabs rather than hard-shelled prawns. In terms of texture and taste, however, they are closer to large prawns than to crabs, and in some recipes they can be substituted for prawns and, more importantly perhaps, vice versa. Accordingly, there are a number of references to this quartet in the text, though this is a prawn companion not a lobster companion. Because of the confusion between crawfish and crayfish, and because Dublin Bay prawns are not prawns at all, I have adopted the following nomenclature:

Scampo (plural scampi) for Dublin Bay prawn, langoustine
  (French), Norway lobster or *Nephrops norvegicus*
Écrevisse for fresh-water crayfish, crawfish (US), *Astacus astacus*
Langouste for salt-water crawfish, spiny lobster (i.e. clawless),
  Palinurus elephas, Palinurus vulgaris.

Travellers in Europe should bear in mind that while *langoustines* are scampi in French, *langostinos* are large prawns, not scampi, in Spanish.

Fresh Prawns or Frozen?

Whenever possible, prawns should be purchased alive and kicking, for like almost all fish (except skate) the fresher they are the better. For most people most of the time this advice is impossible to follow. It is very difficult to buy live or freshly dead prawns these days. Sometimes, locally caught specimens can be found in remote little non-commercialised fishing villages, and live specimens are sometimes to be had in French and Spanish markets, but prawns (unlike lobsters) soon perish when removed from their natural environment – and when dead they deteriorate faster than other fish. Stored on ice or under refrigeration, whole fresh prawns will keep for three or four days; at 60°F they only have one day; at 80°F (as in the tropics) a few hours. If decapitated when caught, they keep longer, since the stomach and digestive system, principal causes of decay, are in the head.

For centuries, all prawns not immediately consumed were sun dried and often turned into dried shrimp paste (balachan, trasi, and so on) wherever it was hot enough to dry them. In cooler climes they were eaten by the locals, transported short distances to inland towns and cities (farther, of course, with the advent of railways) and consumed as seaside treats by visitors. Around Britain and Ireland, scampi, not meaty enough to bother about, were thrown back into the sea. The deep freeze (preceded by the canning industry) has changed all that.

In general, I am sceptical about the gastronomic benefits of freezing. Frozen pork will not crackle; frozen Cheddar goes granular; frozen peas not only bear scant resemblance to fresh ones, they are not as good as some tinned varieties. Most fish, however, freeze well and prawns are no exception. If frozen quickly and thawed slowly (very important), they are almost as good as fresh ones, and a lot safer than unfrozen prawns which have been around a bit. The freezer, moreover, means that prawns from Greenland's icy mountains and India's coral strand can be bought by the man or woman in the Clapham supermarket.

In Britain, the great majority of frozen prawns are already cooked, and many of them are both cooked and peeled. In the United States, on the other hand, it is easy to obtain frozen, uncooked shrimp. Pre-cooked and peeled prawns are fine for salads, cocktails and garnishes, but less satisfactory for serious cooking than raw ones. They cannot be subjected to culinary heat for longer than a few minutes without deterioration and toughening of texture. After a second cooking, the pleasure of the prawn fades all too quickly. In the recipes which follow, uncooked prawns are preferable for the hot dishes, but because of the difficulty of finding raw ones in many areas, I have usually indicated how the dish can be made with cooked prawns, by holding them back till the final stage.

On the face of it, there is no compelling reason why frozen raw prawns should be so difficult to find in the United Kingdom. They are raw when caught and can perfectly well be frozen in that state. In fact many of them are: North Atlantic prawn trawlers sometimes spend two to four weeks at sea, freezing each catch as it comes aboard. Back in Iceland or Greenland the prawns are thawed by a special process, cooked and refrozen. Most of them are also peeled. These extra processes add to the price and subtract from the utility.

The British prawn industry maintains that there is no demand for uncooked prawns and that they are difficult to market raw because they have less eye appeal than cooked ones. Doubtless it is correct about the lack of demand, but that argument assumes the market is consumer-led and that manufacturers merely respond to public demand – which is demonstrably not the case. In affluent countries there is seldom, if ever, any widespread demand for products which are not in the shops. What happens is that entrepreneurs identify potential gaps in the market, obtain products to fill them, and try to create a demand. As I write, for example, a leading supplier is test marketing 'oven–crisp king prawns – hot and spicy Cajun style' in Britain. Clearly there has never been any spontaneous demand for this product, but the popularity of Cajun cooking in the United States suggests there is a reasonable chance of creating a demand. (Incidentally, I thought they were rather good, but they should be hotter and spicier).

It is my conviction that raw prawns represent a bigger gap in the market than any additional cooked product, however spicy. If American shoppers buy raw prawns, why shouldn't British? After all, the convenience-food explosion has been accompanied – perversely, symbiotically? – by a positive renaissance in real cooking, and if any-thing more so in Britain than the United States.

The eye-appeal argument has a certain force. In general, the greyish translucence of raw prawns is less attractive than the pink and red opacity of their cooked counterparts. With *Pandalus borealis*, however, the colour of both the cooked and the raw prawn is similar. Raw North Atlantic prawns would be more attractive in the freezer cabinet than the Far Eastern competitors which can be found in some Chinese supermarkets.

How This Book is Organised

Prawnography is arranged alphabetically and includes both recipes and general knowledge about prawns. The recipes come from all over the world, but I have not attempted to give all the different Indian and Oriental ways of dealing with crustaceans – because they are legion. The East's range of recipes promises a diversity of taste which it does not, in practice, deliver, delicious though many of them are. I have tried to select Asiatic dishes which are genuinely different from each other rather than minor variations on well-known themes, and I have tried to avoid recipes which call for over-obscure ingredients. Recipe selection also reflects the view that in very many cases Chinese dishes are best left to the craftsmen of – Cathay.

Wherever they come from, many of the recipes are given with precise instructions as to ingredients and methods. Some recipes, where there are a number of variables and options, are guidelines which indicate a general direction and approximate destination, but leave details of the actual route to the cook's discretion. Throughout the book I have assumed that the reader is familiar with the basic grammar of cooking and has access to standard recipe books and a liberal repertoire of spices, herbs, oils, vinegars and condiments.

Relevant cross-reference entries are indicated by the use of SMALL CAPITAL LETTERS.

Publishing details of books cited in the text are given in the Bibliography, page 191.

Weights and Measures; Terminology

As prawn, rather than shrimp, is the term used in the majority of English-speaking countries, it seems appropriate to use imperial weights and measures. For the convenience of converts to metrication, here is a short *aide–mémoire*.

1 oz	28 grams
4 oz	112 grams
16 oz/1 lb	450 grams

½ pint	28 centilitres
1 pint	56 centilitres
1 inch	2·5 centimetres
1 foot	30·5 centimetres
100 grams	3½ oz
500 grams	1 lb 2 oz
1 kilogram	2 lb 3 oz
50 centilitres (5dl)	1 scant pint (0·88 pint)
1 litre	1·76 pints
10 centimetres	3·9 inches

Some Other Conversions
1 pint shrimps = 8 oz (225g) shrimps
1 lb unshelled prawns = just over 8 oz (225g) hand-shelled, de-headed prawns

Helpings
For starters or savouries allow about 2 oz shelled prawns per person. For main courses allow 3½–4 oz weight per person.

Capsicum and Pepper Terminology
Throughout this companion, 'pimento' is used instead of sweet pepper, bell pepper, capsicum, and so on; 'cayenne' is used for chilli powder or hot red pepper; sweet red pepper is called 'paprika'. 'Pepper' means black pepper; white pepper is always so written.

Contractions
Tablespoonful is shortened to 'tab', teaspoonful to 'tsp' and dessertspoonful to 'dsp'.

The
Prawnographic
A–Z

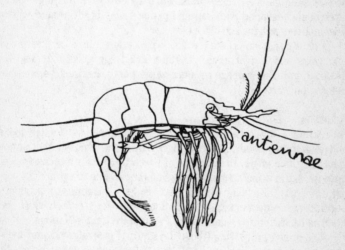

antennae

Abdomen

Prawns are divided into abdomens and carapaces – or heads and tails, the terminology normally used in this book. The abdomen is the part which is eaten, though the carapace, very useful for soups and stocks, is also edible. A defining characteristic of all shrimps and prawns is that the shell which covers the tail has exactly six segments.

Acetes japonicus

A very small, shallow-water marine shrimp indigenous to the Indian Ocean and western Pacific. It is fished by the billion and made into shrimp paste, an important condiment in many Asian cuisines. See BALACHAN.

Acorda Marisco

This is a sort of Portuguese prawn porridge. A loaf of white bread is soaked in water, squeezed out and beaten up with olive oil, egg yolks and crushed garlic. Peeled prawns are added to the mixture which, after being seasoned with salt and pepper, may be decorated with a few unpeeled prawns and black olives.

For a large, de-crusted white loaf, allow about 8 oz prawns, 3 egg yolks and ¼ pint olive oil. Hard-boiled egg yolks may also be incorporated. But squeeze as much water out of the bread as possible before you start.

Additives

An additive is 'any substance not normally consumed as a food by itself and not normally used as a typical ingredient of the food, whether or not it has nutritive value, the addition of which to food for a technological purpose in the manufacture, processing preparation, treatment, packing, transport, or holding of such food results … in it or its by-products becoming a component of … such foods'. *Codex Alimentaris* of the Food and Agriculture Organisation (FAO) of the United Nations.

The prawn-processing (these days mostly freezing) industry uses phosphates and sulphites. SODIUM TRIPOLYPHOSPHATE helps to keep moisture in the prawns and prevent weight loss, thus preserving the original appearance; SODIUM BISULPHITE inhibits MELANOSIS. In the correct dosage these chemicals are harmless, indeed beneficial. Practices and regulations vary from country to country. The United States, for example, limits the permitted concentration of sodium bisulphite to one part per hundred thousand (100 mg per kg) in the edible portion of the shrimp.

Another additive, though it does not quite fit the *Codex* definition, is water itself. To preserve their shape and to protect them from freezer burn, prawns, and peeled prawns in particular, are coated with a thin layer of ice. This, of course, must add a little to their weight. However, it is simple enough for an unscrupulous processor to add a thick or very thick layer of ice and thereby greatly increase the 'weight' of each prawn. Packs which yield 25 per cent to 40 per cent water (and not very nice water at that) are by no means uncommon. At these levels, each 1 lb pack produces 8–12 oz of prawn or less. In Britain the industry is now setting its house in order, and reputable brands increasingly state the full defrosted weight on their packs. These are the ones to buy if you resent paying prawn prices for water. A 1 lb pack which claims to yield 14 oz prawns is likely to be trustworthy.

Aguacete Relleno con Seviche de Camarones

This is a Mexican improvement on the somewhat over-exposed prawns and avocado starter.

> 8 oz shelled prawns
> ¼ pint fresh lime or lemon juice
> 1 tomato, peeled and chopped
> 1 red pimento, chopped finely
> 1 fresh chilli, cut in fine strips
> 1 tab fresh CORIANDER or parsley, chopped
> 2 spring onions
> 6 olives
> 4 tabs olive oil or vegetable oil
> Salt and pepper
> 2 ripe avocados

Marinate prawns in lime juice for 2–3 hours. Before serving, add tomato, pimento, chilli, coriander, chopped spring onion, halved or quartered olives (stoneless), oil, salt and pepper. Toss the resulting mixture, and spoon it into halved avocados.

A la Crème

This is one of the simplest and most elegant ways of preparing crusta-ceans for the table, whether they are pre-cooked or raw. Detailed recipes are given later (see CREVETTES), but the engagingly flexible basic formula is worth noting here. First, heat or cook the prawns in a little butter; second, flare them with brandy or some other fiery spirit; third, cover them with cream, season with salt and pepper and bring the dish briefly to the boil. Serve on a little rice or a big mushroom.

Adaptations or additions can include parsley, dill, lemon or lime juice, paprika, ginger, garlic, Pernod.

With small-to-medium sized prawns, this makes an excellent starter; with large ones or lobster it provides a main course which is rich without overtaxing the digestion.

Alabama Sauce

A mayonnaise-based sauce which is piquantly compatible with cold prawns or almost any seafood platter. To ½ pint mayonnaise add:

> 1 red or green pimento, chopped finely
> 1 clove of garlic, peeled and crushed
> 1 red or green chilli, seeded and chopped finely
> 1 oz grated horseradish
> 2 tabs tomato chutney (ketchup if you prefer)
> 2 tabs cream

The quantities are not mandatory. In particular, the chilli, garlic and horseradish elements may be increased or decreased according to taste, though they must not be omitted. The tomato chutney could be replaced by ripe, peeled tomatoes, to a purée whizzed in a blender. This is one of the mixtures where a good proprietary mayonnaise is a sensible time-saver.

Anatomy

Like all crustacea, prawns and shrimps have segmented bodies. The segments, or somites, are essentially simple rings each of which has one pair of APPENDAGES, such as legs. The somites overlap each other to form an external skeleton, known in the trade as an exoskeleton (all decapods, of course, are invertebrate).

Made of calcium-rich CHITIN, the rings are continuous over the whole body, but are jointed. At joints the chitin may be thin and soft, permitting the parts to move upon one another, as in the tail, thereby enabling them to swim. Elsewhere the somites are fused together, as in the prawn's head, and their separate origins are only demonstrated by the appendages. Where there is more than one pair of appendages, there must be more than one somite. The head, for example, consists of five somites fused together and has ten appendages: two pairs of ANTENNAE (feelers); one pair of mandibles (jaws proper); two pairs of maxillae (accessory jaws). However, the head is fused to the thorax, which has another eight fused segments and sixteen appendages: three pairs of maxillipeds (jaw feet), five pairs of pereiopods (the ten legs which make prawns 'decapods').

The abdomen has six supple, jointed somites, five of them furnished with pairs of pleopods (for swimming), and one, the last, with uropods (part of the tail fan, or steering mechanism). This makes the total of nineteen somites which is common to all prawns and shrimps.

Antennae
Prawns have two pairs of antennae, though in many species one pair is much longer than the other. Their prime function is sensory, though in all probability they also act as part of the balancing mechanism for swimming. In some crustacea (not prawns) the antennae are important organs of locomotion, sexual 'claspers', or agents of parasitic attachment.

Appendages
The collective word for the legs, claws, antennae, flagellae, pleopods and so on of crustacea. A curious attribute of these appendages is that if removed, say by accident or in a fight, or experimentally, they grow again. However, they do not necessarily grow quite as well. If a lobster, for example, loses its larger claw, the new one that replaces it will be the smaller claw, and the claw which was previously inferior becomes superior.

Aquaculture of Prawns
In Ecuador they tell a story about how prawn farming began. During the late 1960s, at a time when the world banana market was at rock bottom, the owners of a large plantation decided to root out all their banana trees and try a different crop. The plantation occupied flat, low-lying land near the Pacific, and no sooner had the trees been removed than a freak tide inundated the coastal plain. When the waters receded they left behind hundreds of pools, thanks to the holes vacated by the banana trees – and the holes were full of baby PENAEUS VANNAMEI, or cameron blanco (Ecuador), or WHITELEG SHRIMP (United States). The white shrimp throve on the natural food supply in their lukewarm baths, augmented no doubt by occasional titbits from passers-by, and in a few months' time were six to nine inches long – ready for the pot.

Well, the story probably has some basis in fact, and Ecuador is certainly now becoming less of a banana republic than a shrimp state. It has the right conditions for a branch of farming which needs plenty of water, plenty of heat and plenty of suitable land. After a slow and sketchy start, prawn or shrimp farming is developing around the equatorial world into a significant business, even if it is still far from being an exact science. Ecuador is one of the leaders, along with Mexico and Taiwan. Shrimp and prawn farms are also hard currency earners for Bangladesh, the Philippines, Malaysia and Indonesia. China is showing interest, as are a number of Middle Eastern countries. (Southern Israel would be a good location, but Israelites are only allowed to eat fish with scales and fins.)

The farm I visited near Guayaquil has some 2,000 acres under water. It is one of the larger shrimp farms in the country, but by no means the largest. Just over three feet deep, the ponds are quadrilateral and about the size of large fields. They have all had to be excavated by hand or digger, and are divided by sturdy banks, not unlike Dutch dykes, which are wide enough to take a Land-rover.

A canal, fed from a tidal estuary, supplies the water, salinity and acidity being regularly checked. Each pond has its own inlets and outlets. One pond is stocked with wild larvae, the others with post-larval shrimp from the larvae pond.

Since there is insufficient natural food, both shrimp and larvae are fed artificial foods from boats; the very largest farms are beginning to feed from the air, using microlights.

It takes up to six months for the wild larvae, microscopic when first caught, to grow to one centimetre in length and one gram in weight – the approximate stage at which they are transferred to the main ponds. Thereafter they grow fast, reaching on average a very marketable four to six inches in about four months. Some tropical species, however, achieve maturity within 208 days of hatching.

If they survive, predators, whether winged, aquatic or human, are a constant problem. As you approach the farm, you divine that it is already a favourite restaurant for the white heron. At the ponds themselves, charming swallow-like patelatas swoop and plunge, swim and duck-dive in search of a snack. On the banks, men lurk with shotguns and fishing tackle. It is easy enough to shoot a heron, but the patelata, surely the prettiest of predators, must be as difficult to hit as snipe or woodcock. Often, too, the tidal waters let in fish, even lobsters, which make pigs of themselves on the tender young prawns until they are caught by the marksmen.

Man is the worst problem, as usual. Whether for sale or for supper, *Penaeus vannamei* are tempting morsels. Of the seventy people who work on this farm, thirty-one are police or security personnel.

Technologically, the farm described is intermediate. Others are smaller and simpler, essentially cottage industries. In some places, prawn farming still consists of flooding a coastal plot when hatched natural larvae are abundant, and letting the captured babes fend for themselves for all or most of their food. For social and humanitarian reasons it is to be hoped that aquatic peasant farming will be able to co-exist with more capital-intensive forms. The shortage of wild larvae is often a problem.

High-tech shrimp farming is where the future more probably lies. It is now possible to hatch the eggs artificially, and feasible to rear as many as 200,000 prawns per hectare, as opposed to the 60,000 which is a good average for intermediate aquafarms today. As yet, attempts to breed prawns in captivity have met with limited success, but the industry is confident this problem will be overcome. Until it is, the short supply of wild larvae – catching large quantities of such microscopic matter is a highly specialised occupation – will limit the industry's development. All the other stages of prawns' life cycle are being subjected to increasingly tight and market-oriented control. How will the quality survive – will prawns go the way of battery chickens?

Farmed prawn today stand up pretty well in comparison with wild, though fair comparison of like with like is almost impossible, if the wild prawns are fresh and the farmed ones frozen. Perhaps the best guarantee that present standards will be maintained or improved would be to insist that farmed prawns should be labelled as such.

The principal species being farmed today are PENAEUS VANNAMEI (Pacific white or whiteleg shrimp), PENAEUS MONODON (giant tiger prawn, the largest commercial species), and MACROBRACHIUM ROSENBERGII (giant river prawn, a fresh-water species).

Arastaeomorpha foliacea

The giant red prawn or gamba roja, found in temperate latitudes on both sides of the North Atlantic and in the Mediterranean; also in south-east African waters. Highly esteemed for its taste, especially by the French and Spanish, and consequently in short supply. It grows to about nine inches and turns red when cooked.

Aristeus antennatus

Except that it has a bluish head when alive, this is similar to the giant red prawn, and often caught with it. It is found in deep water in the Mediterranean, and off the Atlantic coasts of Spain, Portugal and West Africa, but not on the other side of the Atlantic. It grows to eight inches if given the chance.

Aristotle

Greek polymath (384 – 322 BC) who first realised that observation was the basis of natural science. Accordingly, he observed that 'Crustacea [the crayfish, the lobsters, the prawns] copulate as the RETROMINGENT quadruped – when one animal turns its tail supine and the other prone. They copulate in early spring, near the land. This can be asserted, for the copulation of all creatures of this sort has been observed. Sometimes it occurs when the figs begin to ripen'. *Historia Animalum*, Book V.

Arroz a la Marinara

An all-seafood paella variant in which prawns have a supporting role. For 6 people:

> 1½ lb good white fish such as haddock, monkfish, turbot (may be mixed)
> White wine
> Olive oil
> Onion, peeled and chopped
> 8 oz squid
> Paprika
> 14 oz rice
> Bay leaf
> Saffron
> Garlic, peeled
> 18 mussels in their shells
> 18 prawns in their shells

Make 1¾ pints of fish stock with the bones, trimmings and heads of white fish, using white wine as well as water.

Heat 3 tabs oil in a large shallow pan or ovenproof dish and melt the onion in it for 5–6 minutes; add the fish and squid cut in chunks, and brown slightly, shaking in 1 dsp Spanish paprika. Turn the fish over gently. Remove the fish when it is about half cooked, but leave squid in pan. Add the rice and let it fry in the oil, stirring it enough to coat each grain at least notionally – about 90 seconds. Then add the strained stock – it should be twice the volume of the rice (measure both in a large mug, if you like). Bring the whole up to simmering point. Add the bay leaf and a good pinch of saffron (or 1 tsp turmeric – the final dish does need to be yellow) and insert 2–6 cloves garlic according to the strength of your addiction. Float the mussels, washed and de-bearded but still in their shells, on the top. Cover the pan and barely simmer for 10 minutes. Add the prawns, if they are uncooked, and cook for a further 10 minutes, uncovered. Watch the rice carefully at this stage. The dish is ready when all the liquid is absorbed.

If using pre-cooked prawns, delay their introduction to the rice until 5 minutes before serving the dish.

The Spanish use a round, risotto-type rice for this sort of dish, but long-grain rice can be substituted.

Arroz de Camaroes

1 lb unshelled prawns
1 pint milk
Bay leaf
Thyme
2 onions, chopped finely, or the equivalent in shallots
2 red or green pimentos, seeded and sliced finely
Olive oil
Butter
Flour
6 TOMATOES, peeled and chopped finely
Salt and pepper
Parsley
2 tabs cream (optional)

Simmer the heads and shells of the prawns in milk with a small bay leaf and a sprig of thyme for 10–15 minutes. Then strain the milk and put to one side.

Gently fry the onions in a mixture of olive oil and butter, and add the pimentos after a few minutes. When they are soft but not brown, add enough flour to absorb the frying medium and form a light ROUX. Add the prawn-flavoured milk little by little, eliminating lumps with a wooden spoon. Then add the tomatoes, and simmer for 15 minutes, stirring frequently. Next add the prawns, if raw. If they are cooked, let the sauce continue to cook for another 10 minutes before adding them. Season with salt and pepper. When the prawns are cooked (or heated through), finish the dish with a good tablespoonful of chopped parsley and a little cream. Serve with plain boiled rice.

Astacus astacus
See ÉCREVISSE.

Ayam Petis

A prawn-accented chicken casserole from Indonesia, calling for prawn or shrimp paste and prawn or shrimp sauce, both of which are readily found in oriental stores. Lemon grass is less widely available, but can be found in Thai emporia and sometimes in large supermarkets.

1 large onion, peeled and chopped
3 cloves garlic, peeled and chopped
1 tsp fresh ginger, chopped finely
Peanut oil
3 fresh chillies, chopped
1 tsp turmeric
1 tsp crushed black peppercorns
1½ tsps TRASI (dried shrimp paste)
3-in length lemon grass
1 tab prawn sauce
Salt
3 lb roasting chicken cut into 8 pieces
½ pint COCONUT MILK
1 tab molasses, dark brown sugar, or palm sugar
1 tab lemon juice

Fry onion, garlic and ginger in peanut oil. When the onion is soft, add chillies and turmeric, black peppercorns and shrimp paste. Fry for 1 minute. Add lemon grass (lemon rind can be substituted, but it does not have the same aromatic subtlety), prawn sauce (or concentrated prawn stock), salt and chicken pieces. Cook for 5 minutes before adding the coconut milk and sugar. Simmer with lid off for half an hour, or a little longer, till the chicken is tender and the sauce pleasantly thick. At the last minute add lemon juice and give the casserole a good stir.

B

-Balachong-

-S. Indian Pickle-

Baconed Prawns

Interesting starter or savoury. Best with large, fat prawns, but can be adumbrated with smaller ones or even shrimps.

> Shelled prawns (pre-cooked are fine), about 2 oz per person
> Lemon juice
> Olive oil
> Paprika
> Pepper
> Mixed herbs
> Streaky bacon, cut thin

Toss the prawns in lemon juice and olive oil, and season them with paprika, pepper and mixed herbs. Leave for at least 15 minutes, preferably about 1 hour.

Wrap each prawn in half a rasher of streaky bacon and fasten it with a wooden toothpick. Bake them in a very hot oven for 6–7 minutes. Serve on hot buttered toast.

If using small prawns or shrimps, make a parcel of them big enough for the bacon to enfold.

If serving baconed prawns as a savoury, substitute cayenne for paprika and dust one side of the bacon with mustard powder.

Baked Prawns

Can be made with whole or shelled prawns, small or medium, cooked or raw. If the prawns are pre-cooked, minimise the re-cooking by finishing the dish under a fierce grill. For 4 people as a starter.

> 8 oz prawns or shrimps
> ¼ pint dry white wine or dry cider
> Salt and pepper
> ½ oz butter
> 2 tabs breadcrumbs
> 1 clove garlic, peeled and crushed
> 1 leek, chopped finely and blanched in boiling water

Put the prawns in a fireproof dish and moisten them with white wine or cider. Season with salt and pepper, dot with butter.

Mix the breadcrumbs with crushed garlic and leek. Spread the resulting paste over the prawns and bake for 15–20 minutes in a medium to hot oven if the prawns are uncooked. Otherwise grill till hot right through and carbonised on top.

Baked Stuffed Prawns
For 4 people as a starter.

> Butter
> 20 prawns, peeled and defrosted
> 20 mussels, cockles or clams
> Breadcrumbs
> Salt and pepper
> Lemon juice
> Tabasco
> Spring onions, chopped finely
> Parsley (optional)

Generously butter a shallow fireproof dish. Cover the bottom with prawns so that each pink crescent offers a little space into which you can insert a cockle, mussel or clam, previously rolled in breadcrumbs. Season with salt and pepper, sharpen with lemon juice and tabasco.

Mix more breadcrumbs with spring onion and a little parsley; sprinkle lightly over the prawns. Drizzle melted butter over the crumbs and then add a second crumb sprinkling. Bake in a very hot oven for 6 minutes.

Alternative stuffings: fish or smoked fish mousse; smoked mackerel (cold-smoked if possible).

Balachan, Blachan
A powerful prawn condiment which, with slight variations, is used throughout south-east Asia – in meat, poultry and vegetable cooking, as well as with fish. In effect it is an extra spice. Novices should use it most sparingly.

Balachan is usually made from shrimps rather than prawns. They are salted, dried, pounded and left to rot in a hot, humid environment. As they mature they develop a very strong smell. Eventually they are formed into cakes or cubes and wrapped or otherwise packaged so that the odour is insulated from everyday life.

In cooking, the balachan is either fried with other spices or roasted before being incorporated into a dish. In one form or another it can now be bought in oriental stores or the nearest Chinatown in most parts of the world – varying in colour from pink to red to dark brown to grey.

At a pinch, shrimp paste mixed with water makes instant fish stock.

Synonyms: trasi (Indonesia); ngapi (Burma); kapi (Thailand).

Balachaung

Not the same as BALACHAN, but a Burmese derivative. Ngapi, prawn powder and chilli are mixed to a paste with vinegar, fried till crisp, allowed to cool, mixed with separately fried onion and garlic, and served as an accompaniment to rice. Stored in airtight jars it keeps for weeks.

Balachong

A South Indian pickle made with salted fresh prawns (not rotted ones) plus mangoes, onions and spices. Eaten with curries and so on, and available like other pickles from Indian grocers.

Batter

One of the most popular ways of cooking prawns is to deep-fry them in batter, often with the shell and head removed but with the tail fin left *in situ*. Obviously, it is better to use uncooked prawns for this dish. Here are three good batter recipes.

English Batter

> 1 oz plain flour
> 5 tabs beer or water
> salt

Mix the flour and the beer or water to a smooth, lump-free paste. Add salt and leave it for 20 minutes before using it to coat the prawns.

Japanese batter

> 1 egg
> 1 cup ice-cold water
> Bicarbonate of soda
> ¾ cup unsifted flour

Break egg into the water and whisk until frothy. Add a pinch of bicarbonate of soda and the flour. Mix well without overbeating. If the batter still seems thick, add a little more cold water.

A third variant is to use 1 egg, 4 oz flour, ½ pint water. Whisk the ingredients with a chopstick while the oil is heating and use the batter straight away.

See also WHITE OF EGG.

Béarnaise Sauce

This cold version of the classic sauce goes very well with prawns, langoustines or lobster, and makes a pleasant change from mayonnaise. The fresh tarragon is important.

 1 or 2 shallots, peeled and chopped
 Glass white wine plus 1 tab tarragon vinegar
 3 egg yolks
 5–6 tabs olive oil (or olive and sunflower oil mixed)
 Fresh tarragon
 Salt and pepper

Boil the shallots in the wine and vinegar until the liquid is reduced to 2 tabs. Remove the shallots and cool the liquor. Beat the egg yolks into the liquor, and start adding the oil very slowly, almost drop by drop, over a very low heat. As you add the oil, beat the mixture with a wooden spoon to a creamy consistency. Finally add chopped tarragon, salt and pepper.

 3 egg yolks can take considerably more oil than is indicated above.

 The sauce can be eaten hot as well as cold (but I prefer butter for the hot version).

Béchamel Sauce

Béchamel, the basic white sauce of the European kitchen, is frequently used in hot prawn dishes. Melted butter is mixed with flour in varying quantities, depending upon how thick you wish the sauce to be, over a medium heat to make a ROUX. Heated milk is added little by little (and sometimes FISH STOCK too). 2 oz roux will take roughly 1 pint liquid. Quantities and proportions can be varied depending on how thick you wish the finished sauce to be. The tendency to form lumps at first must be thwarted with a wooden spoon, but once the paste has changed from thick to thin the milk can be added more quickly. The sauce must then be cooked till it re-thickens. Béchamels should be well seasoned, and many people would say that the inclusion of a bay leaf is mandatory.

Beurre Blanc Sauce

Very good with hot, freshly boiled prawns, ÉCREVISSES or LANGOUSTINES; a useful alternative to drawn or melted butter for boiled lobster.

 1 shallot or 2–3 spring onions, chopped roughly
 ¼ pint dry white wine and vinegar mixed
 8 oz unsalted butter

1 tab cream (optional)
Salt and pepper

Boil the spring onions or shallot in wine and vinegar, reducing the mixture to 2 tabs. Discard onion. Cool liquor a little by transferring it to another saucepan. Over a very low heat add the butter, cold and cut into cubes, stirring continuously. After adding the first 2–3 pieces of butter, try adding a small spoonful of cream – though not absolutely kosher, this helps, I find, to bind the sauce. Then go back to the butter, adding it cube by cube, stirring the while. Finish with a little more cream if you like.

The incorporation of a little home-made tomato sauce is mildly heretical but rather good with DECAPODA NATANTIA.

Bisque de Crevettes

Bisques are rich, fulfilling soups which can be made with lobster, langouste, prawns, crab, even the modest shrimp. Essential ingredients include white wine, rice and cream; essential processes include pounding or blending the crustacean meat, and pounding the shells and heads.

1 onion and 2 carrots, peeled and diced as for a mirepoix
Butter
1½lb whole prawns, large and uncooked for preference
2 tabs brandy
Large glass dry white wine
2 pints FISH STOCK or chicken stock
3 oz rice
¼ pint cream
½ tsp cayenne pepper

Sauté the mirepoix in butter until the vegetables begin to brown. Add the washed prawns and cook for 5 minutes. Add 1 tab warm brandy and ignite; then add the white wine and ½ pint stock. Remove the prawns, trying not to burn your fingers, and leave the liquor simmering gently.

Meanwhile, in another saucepan, overboil the rice in the remainder of the fish or chicken stock. Cook it to a creamy consistency – about 25 minutes.

Peel the prawns. Pound the heads and shells in a mortar and return them to the simmering broth (or, if you like, the stock in which the rice is boiling). The shells should have at least a further 15 minutes cooking.

Pound or blend the prawn meat with 2 oz softened butter and ½ tsp cayenne pepper.

Add the rice liquor to the mirepoix liquor, and when the prawn shells have been cooked long enough to have their essence extracted, strain and rub the mixture through a fine sieve.

Re-heat, adding the cream and the prawn meat. Simmer for at least 5 minutes. Before being served, the soup may again be sieved, but this is unnecessary. More to the point is to add the remaining table-spoon of brandy. If available, 1 tsp PRAWN BUTTER should be added to each helping.

If using cooked prawns, the initial frying should be reduced to 2 minutes.

Blackened Cajun Shrimp

This version comes from Greg Morton, former jazz musician in New Orleans and now proprietor of the Bridge Street Café, South Dartmouth, Massachusetts. It involves a blackening mixture – which can be made in bulk and stored in an airtight jar for several weeks – or given to friends as a present.

5 tabs paprika
2 pulverised bay leaves
2 tsps each oregano, basil, thyme, salt, white pepper,
1 tsp cayenne or 2 tsps Szechuan pepper, if you have it.

Mix all ingredients thoroughly with a whisk. They will blacken any fish fowl or meat. Now take:

4–5 large shrimps per person, peeled and deveined, tails on
Blackening mixture
Clarified butter or GHEE

You also need a cast-iron pan (skillet) – aluminium or steel will not do – and pastry brush. Metal skewers are not essential but are a good way of handling the shrimp while cooking them. *It is imperative that your kitchen has good ventilation because this cooking technique produces a great deal of smoke.*

Dredge the shrimp thoroughly with the blackening mixture. If using skewers, push them, once loaded, into the spice, then flip over and repeat. Using the pastry brush, sprinkle the prawns liberally with hot clarified butter.

Heat the pan so that it is very hot indeed – no oil, butter or fat. Put the shrimps on to the pan and press them down with a metal spatula so that as much shrimp as possible touches the cooking surface. Cook for 3–4 minutes on each side.

This recipe may be performed on a very hot charcoal grill, omitting the iron plate, with frequent butter basting.

Boiled Eggs

Freshly boiled shrimps
Butter
Fresh eggs, large

Peel the shrimps – about 8 per egg. Bisect them and warm them through in butter. Meanwhile, lightly boil the eggs.

Decapitate the eggs, and discard the white from the lids. Fill each lid with buttery shrimps. Put the eggs into egg cups. Replace the lids deftly so that all shrimps are enclosed.

Eat with teaspoons, fingers of toast and black pepper.

Potted shrimps may be used for this little treat.

Boiled Prawns

A simple Japanese method for uncooked prawns, whole or deheaded.

12 large prawns, washed
4 tabs SOY sauce
4 tabs water
1 tab medium sherry (or mirin)

Remove prawn heads if necessary. Combine soy, water and sherry. Bring to boil, adding prawns. Cook for about 5 minutes. Extract the prawns and put them in a warm bowl. Transfer cooking liquor to another bowl and use it as a dipping sauce.

Boric Acid

H_3BO_3 was widely used for the preservation of shellfish and other foods for many years. For example, Spanish trawlermen fishing off the Moroccan coast for several weeks at a time used boric acid to preserve each day's catch. Their technique was to put the prawns on ice, dust them with (powdered) boric acid, add more ice, more prawns, more acid, and so on in layers. This practice prevented MELANOSIS and the shellfish were preserved perfectly until unloaded in port. However, boric acid is no longer permitted as a food preservative in the European Community and in many other countries.

Its use was discontinued because of general unease about the possible long-term effects of borate ingestion. Uncontrolled application of the preservative could conceivably lead to cases of acute intoxication, since the human body may not be able to eliminate borates rapidly enough if the kidney function is overloaded. Borates, in fact, have relatively low mammalian toxicity (of the same order of magnitude as common salt), and no case of intoxication arising from their use as food preservatives has ever been reported.

The fact that boric acid exerts a powerful bacteriostatic action is the key to its effectiveness as a preservative, but it does not kill salmonella and other bacteria which cause food poisoning. Therefore, its preservative action may disguise the off-flavours and odours which are early-warning signals of food contamination. Arguably this is a more cogent reason for discontinuing the use of what is still the best melanosis inhibitor and shellfish preservative than the possibility of collywobbles arising from something which is only as toxic as the salt we use every day in cooking and on our food.

Bouillabaisse

Fish stews approximating to, or deriving from, the great Marseillaise experience are notably enhanced by the inclusion of prawns. Experts claim that a real bouillabaisse is impossible without rascasse, but experts are often bores.

For a good near-bouillabaisse obtain 3 lb mixed sea fish, about 20 mussels in their shells, and 1 lb uncooked prawns. The fish should not include herring or mackerel, and about one-third should be a firm-fleshed species such as turbot, monkfish or brill. Proceed along these lines: in a large pan, fry peeled and chopped onion and garlic in olive oil; add several peeled and chopped TOMATOES; after 5 minutes add the fish, gutted and scaled, but with bones and skin. Large fish should be cut into medium-sized pieces. Add a glass of white wine and enough water to cover the fish easily, plus a small bunch of parsley, bay leaf, and thyme, saffron and some more olive oil. Boil for 12–14 minutes. Then add prawns and mussels (washed and bearded). Cook for another 6–7 minutes.

Serve the stew in large bowls with a pungent ROUILLE (for which all recipes insist on bread (occasionally potatoes), olive oil and garlic, but some also include anchovies, paprika, olives, pimentoes, chillies, mayonnaise, FISH STOCK and other items).

Bourride

Proceed as for BOUILLABAISSE, but when they are cooked carefully remove all the prawns, mussels and pieces of fish, also the bunch of herbs. Allow the soup remaining in the pan to cool a little, then combine it with an aïoli (garlic mayonnaise made with a relatively large quantity of egg yolks). The best way to marry the two is to loosen the aïoli with a few tablespoonsful of soup before adding it to the remainder of the soup. After that the soup should be cooked over a very, very low heat until it thickens. Then it should be poured over the fish and shellfish which are waiting, one hopes, in a large, warm tureen.

Brine

The typical supermarket prawn – cooked, peeled, frozen – has to be bathed in brine at the processing factory. This points up a flaw in the processing itself. Cooking and peeling apparently leave the prawns relatively tasteless, so taste has to be added artificially. To my mind this strengthens the argument in favour of freezing prawns in their uncooked state. Cooking and peeling make them fast food convenience products – uncooked, unpeeled they scale higher in the gourmet league.

Butter

See PRAWN BUTTER.

Buttered Shrimps

Stew 1 lb shrimps in ½ pint white wine, with nutmeg. Beat 4 eggs and stir 4 oz melted butter into them. Allow the shrimps to cool a little, before adding the egg and butter mixture. Then cook and stir over a very low flame until a further slight thickening takes place. Serve with sippets of toast or fried bread.

A similar dish can be made with prawns, but they have to be shelled.

(*Adapted from a recipe of 1710, quoted in Sheila Hutchins,* English Recipes.)

C

"chelate"
~to have claws~

~claws of shrimp with
brush hairs for
Catching small organisms~

Cabbage
See DALNA.

Cajun blackening mixture
See BLACKENED CAJUN SHRIMP.

Calories
On average there are some 90–100 calories per medium-sized portion
(3½ oz) of prawns.

Camaroes com Vinho do Porto

> 8 oz shelled prawns
> 2 oz butter
> 2 medium onions, peeled and chopped
> 2 tabs dry port (white or a light tawny)
> 8 egg yolks
> 2 tabs cream
> Salt and pepper

Bisect or, if large, quarter the prawns. Fry the onions in butter until
they are soft and golden. Add the prawns and cook gently for 4–5
minutes (if raw) or 1 minute if pre-cooked. Add the port and let it
bubble for a minute or two, deglazing the butter.

Beat the egg yolks with the cream, and season with salt and pepper.
Allow the onion and prawn mixture to cool a little, then add it to the egg
mixture. Pour the combination into 4 individual ramekins and bake in a
medium-low oven until the eggs have set, about 15 minutes.

Cameroon
Country in West Africa whose name derives from the Portuguese
word for prawn. The story goes that in the late fifteenth century
King Henry the Navigator's fleet reached an African cape where the
water was pink. Edging closer they found that the bay was seething
with shrimp. 'Camaroes' exclaimed the Admiral, giving orders for
supper. To this day that peninsula is called Cabo de Camaraõs,
the river is Rio de Camaraõs, and the country, once a French and
before that a German colony, is now called Cameroon. See NUPTIAL
SWARMING.

Is it possible that the Cameron clan in Scotland can claim the same
etymology? I think not, for according to Moule's *Heraldry of Fish* the
only family with prawns in its coat of arms is the Atseas of Kent (barry

wavy of six, or and gules, three prawns naiant in the first and of the second).

Cannibalism
Prawns, like lobsters, are shamelessly, but not exclusively, cannibalistic. When short of food they eat each other without qualm, but if there is adequate alternative nourishment they respect each other's decapodan rights. They also eat their own discarded shells.

The artificial feeds used in aquaculture sometimes contain a proportion of shrimp heads.

Cappon Magro
An elaborate and expensive seafood salad from Genoa, based on lobsters, prawns, crab and oysters. Other ingredients are potatoes, carrots, artichokes, beetroot, cauliflower, French beans, anchovies, olives, white fish such as sea bass – and ship's biscuit. The dressing is made of garlic, parsley, eggs, capers, anchovies, fennel and breadcrumbs, as well as olive oil and vinegar.

Brave spirits who wish to attempt this symposium – a distant cousin of Olde England's salmagundy? – are directed to Elizabeth David's *Italian Food*.

Caramote
French for the very large prawns found in Mediterranean and nearby Atlantic waters. The principal species, PENAEUS KERATHURUS, is considered the best of all prawns, even the best of all crustaceans, by some authorities.

Carapace
The shell over the prawn's cephalothorax, in other words its head; but the carapace contains the vital organs and stomach as well as the head proper.

Caridea
An infra-order of crustacea that include the common shrimp, the North Atlantic prawn and most fresh-water prawns. In caridean species the second segment of the tail overlaps both the first and third segments, whereas in all the penaeids the first segment overlaps the second, the second overlaps the third, and so on.

About 20 per cent of prawns which reach the market are caridean, the rest belong to the PENAEIDEA.

Ceviche (or Seviche)

A west coast South American dish for which fillets of raw fish are marinated in lemon and/or lime juice instead of being cooked. When applied to prawns, however, the fish are sometimes cooked lightly before being marinated. Prawn ceviche is an apotheosis (there are others) of the PRAWN COCKTAIL.

Marinate small to medium prawns in lemon juice along with some sliced onion, garlic and fresh chilli for 4 hours.

Make a piquant tomato dressing by chopping TOMATOES and whizzing them in a blender with chopped red pimentos, then simmering them with a little oil plus sugar, salt, pepper and tabasco for 30 minutes in a covered saucepan. Strain the dressing through a sieve, and allow it to cool.

Add the marinade to the tomato dressing. Serve the prawns on a bed of shredded lettuce with onion rings and strips of red or green pimento, the dressing poured over them, and with a wedge of lemon. Clearly, fresh limes can be used instead of lemon. Additional strong olive oil may be added to the dressing at the final stage, but taste it first for seasoning.

See also MARINATED PRAWNS.

Chelate

Impressive prawnographical term for 'having claws'. Lobsters and prawns are chelate, but langoustes are not. (Our cat is chelate too.)

Chilli, Cayenne Pepper

Prawns have a brazen affinity for, and a notorious susceptibility to, chillies and hot red peppers in all their forms. Hurrah. The serious prawnophile will have fresh chillies in the larder, as well as dried ones, tabasco, chilli powder, paprika and probably some other proprietary condiments based on chilli, such as SAMBAL OELEK.

Chitin

Hornlike integument secreted by the skin which forms the exoskeleton of prawns and other crustaceans. With the empirical formula $C_{15}H_{26}O_{10}N_2$ it can be soft and supple (as at the tail joints) or be hardened by deposition of carbonates and other lime salts.

As you would expect, chitin decomposes into acetic acid and glucosamine if it is boiled in concentrated hydrochloric acid.

Choice of prawns

Consumers may be offered at least twelve forms of shrimp or prawn when they go shopping, though in England they are more likely to be offered only two.

Live Prawns   Gastronomically these are the best raw material to use. They are also the most difficult to market, and in practice almost unobtainable. Certain species survive out of water longer than others, and can live for relatively long periods if packed in damp seaweed. Farmed giant river prawns are being exported live in small quantities to Japan from south-east Asia. It is to be hoped that this trade will increase and spread to Europe.

Whole Fresh Prawns   Most prawns die soon after they are removed from the watery environment, and thereafter deteriorate rapidly. On ice they remain good for forty-eight hours or even a little longer. Whole fresh prawns are found in places where they are appreciated, notably Spain, France, Italy and certain parts of the United States. I have seen them in London's Chinese quarter and at Harrods. It is safest to buy them in shops or markets which have a predictable demand and/or a local source of supply.

Fresh Tails   Since the decay organisms in the stomach and the digestive system are located at the back of the head, prawns keep fresh longer if the head is removed before deterioration begins. Especially in hot weather, it may be advisable to buy fresh tails rather than whole prawns, even if their appearance is not quite so attractive.

Frozen   A very high percentage of the commercial prawn catch all over the world is now frozen, including nearly all exports and imports. Like it or not, most of us have no choice between fresh and frozen, only a choice between different forms of frozen prawn.

If they are quick frozen when in very good condition at an efficient, hygienic plant operated by conscientious personnel, if they are properly handled in the distribution chain, and if they are de-frosted slowly, preferably in a refrigerator, the result, in taste and texture, will be nearly as good as just-caught prawns procured as the fishing boats land and cooked at once. This statement can be made safely since very few people will ever be in a position to test it. Even so, they are rather large ifs. Everyone in the commercial chain wants to make as much money as is compatible with staying in business. Regulations and codes of practice are difficult to formulate or enforce. Prawn-fishing grounds and farms are often located a long way from modern processing facilities. Increasingly, the developed countries rely on Third World suppliers or catches from remote waters hundreds of miles from port or factory. Prawns grow well in the torrid tropics, but the warmth which befriends them in life becomes the enemy once they are on their way to the freezer; and freezer technology, while not particularly high tech by modern standards, is not so simple nor so cheap that all small producers can afford their own, export standard plant.

In Britain there are a number of reputable brands (including supermarket own brands) which are backed by policies of extreme care in terms of quality, hygiene and handling practice. The most common frozen product is the peeled and cooked prawn – one of the less interesting forms from a culinary point of view. It is to be hoped that frozen raw shrimp, as found in the United States, will soon become more widely available. At present it is only found in very up-market fishmongers and specialist outlets such as Chinese supermarkets. Yet if Sainsbury's or Marks & Spencer started promoting and selling raw prawn, the others would soon all follow suit. It has to be admitted that the colour of raw prawns is not as cheerful as the pinks and reds produced by cooking. That is a marketing problem which packaging and design consultants would be happy to solve.

Whole Raw Frozen   Best of the frozen forms, but difficult to find in the United Kingdom. There are genuine problems. One is that after being frozen the prawn APPENDAGES become very brittle, in which state they break off unless handled with great care. One way to preserve their integrity is to freeze the prawns in blocks of ice. Solid blocks can be handled quite roughly without their contents being damaged, an asset in the trade. It is less of an asset in the kitchen since the ice blocks take longer to thaw, and individual prawns cannot be removed from the block at all easily.

Frozen Raw Headless   Internationally this is the most popular form of frozen prawn: head removed but shell and tail fan left intact. When defrosted, they can be cooked as they are; alternatively, shells and tail fan can be removed without trouble. It is said that Americans like this form because it spares them the discomfort and guilt which they feel when they look dead shrimp in the eyes.

Frozen tails of the rock shrimp, found mainly in Florida and the Gulf of Mexico, are usually sold split longitudinally, because their shells are so impenetrable.

Peeled Raw; Peeled and Deveined   Headless, shelled, uncooked prawns with or without the intestinal tract – the 'vein' which carries waste material from the stomach along the back of the tail for excretion. The vein is harmless but does not look very nice, particularly on large prawns, so it is often removed. If it tastes bitter, as is sometimes asserted, the bitterness is extremely subtle. Deveined prawns are more expensive than peeled, undeveined ones. Large prawns are sometimes peeled, deveined and split.

Peeled, Raw, Tail On   This is the form favoured for deep-fried prawns as it enables the diner to convey them to his or her mouth by holding their tails.

Whole Cooked Prawns   One of the commonest forms in British shops; also popular in continental Europe and Japan, but not in the United States. They are usually small or medium-sized prawns, frozen individually rather than in blocks of ice. Those on sale in the United Kingdom are mostly *Pandalus borealis* from the north Atlantic.

Peeled and Cooked   This is the staple product of the prawn trade in Britain. Again the north Atlantic *Pandalus borealis* predominates. No heads, tails or shells; often no veins either, since they are removed in the wash. A trouble-free form, usually of good quality, which is better for salads and prawn cocktails than for hot dishes.

The cheaper, warm-water, peeled and cooked prawns, imported from the East, are inferior in taste and texture, but useful for curries and wok work.

Breaded Prawns   Cooked peeled prawns and scampi are also sold breaded or crumbed. The cheaper forms of breaded 'scampi' may not be whole langoustines at all, but little bits of scampi meat minced up, perhaps with other fish to stretch them, then reformed into a scampi-tail shape. Packets which bear the legend 'individual scampi tails', or words to that effect, should contain the real thing. Breaded prawns can be deep-fried, grilled or baked.

Dried Shrimp   Sun-dried shrimps are one of the ancient food products of the East. The prawns shrivel as they dehydrate and keep almost indefinitely. Cheaper than frozen prawns and easier to store, they are much favoured by ethnic restaurants, but not recommended for good, plain, non-spicy cooking.

Canned Prawns   Once an important product, now rendered

obsolescent by the freezer. Small amounts of the smaller species still go into tins, however. (Canned scampi soup is quite good: could there, perhaps, be a market for canned prawn soup?)

Cholesterol

People who have cholesterol problems have little to fear from prawns unless their intake is habitual and excessive as well as polyunsaturated. The average prawn cholesterol content is about one-third that of eggs – 100 milligrams per 1000 grams, or one part in ten thousand.

Coconut Milk, Coconut Cream

This is used for important prawn dishes in both orient and occident, notably south-east Asia and South America. It is not the water inside a coconut, though that is sometimes incorporated in the preparation process, but a liquor derived front the coconut's flesh. Commercial desiccated coconut is a very good substitute and the obvious thing to use outside the coconut belt.

Put 2 cups desiccated coconut into a large bowl and cover them with 2–3 cups very hot water. When it is lukewarm, knead the coconut, then strain off the thick coconut milk (sometimes called coconut cream at this stage). Repeat the process, using the same coconut, to produce a thinner milk.

Use the cream for recipes which call for it specifically, otherwise combine the two brews.

Using fresh coconut: put 2 cups flesh in an electric blender with 2½ cups warm water. Blend for 30 seconds, then strain off the liquor, squeezing as much out of the nut as possible. Repeat the process with new water and the same coconut.

Coquilles de Crevettes

Prawns
BÉCHAMEL SAUCE
Duchesse (or mashed) potatoes
Grated cheese
Scallop shells

Line the scallop shells with mashed potato to which you have added egg, nutmeg and grated cheese. Pile peeled, cooked prawns within the potato circumference, and cover with béchamel sauce. Sprinkle with grated cheese (and paprika if you like) and grill till brown and bubbly.

'Delicious dish, pity about the ashtrays,' said a friend of mine.

Coriander

Coriandrum sativum is important both as a herb and as a spice. The seed
has an aromatic, faintly orangey flavour and is an important constituent
of curry powders. Used either whole or ground, it is a key spice in Indian
and south-east Asian cooking, its role often being to curb and harmonise
more aggressive ingredients such as pepper and ginger.

Coriander leaf looks rather like French (broad-leaved) parsley. It
has an unmistakable and penetrating flavour – something of an acquired
taste at first, but once acquired compulsive – which bears little relationship to the seed. It is widely used in South American as well as oriental
and Middle Eastern cooking.

Although exotic in the true sense, coriander grows without difficulty out of doors in England, and in fact germinates more easily than
good old umbelliferous parsley.

Court Bouillon

A cooking liquor made with water, white wine (or vinegar sometimes),
onion, garlic, carrot, celery, leek and a herb or two (or bouquet garni).
One or other of the flavourings may be omitted, for example the garlic
or leek; others may be included, for example root fennel. The constitu-
ents are boiled together for about 30 minutes.

Using the strained broth to poach fish or shellfish improves their
flavour. The liquor can subsequently be used as or in a sauce, or it
can form the basis of a soup.

The term NAGE can be treated as a synonym for court bouillon.

Crangon crangon

The common or brown shrimp once found by the billion in the Wash,
Morecambe Bay and off the Wirral. It is still caught, but only in millions.
It may be small, but its flavour is incomparable.

As aphrodisiacs *Crangon crangon*, according to the legendary Mrs
'Arris, are faster acting and more effective than either *Ostrea edulis* or
Homarus gammarus.

The best way to eat fresh-boiled shrimps – with whatever object in
mind – is to hold them by head and tail and bite the bit in the middle.
Head and tail may also be eaten, however, when the shrimps are really
fresh. If they have been kept in a refrigerator overnight after being
cooked, their shells will be shellier and usually too crunchy.

Shelling shrimps quickly is one of the most skilled occupations in the
world, taking something like forty-five years to master. Sexagenarians
in Morecambe and the Wirral used to be able to peel 300 a minute, but
it is a dying art.

Crawfish, Crayfish

Crawfish is the traditional English word for the clawless spiny lobster. But in the United States crawfish usually denotes the small, fresh-water lobster which in England is called crayfish. They manage these things less confusingly in France where the clawless lobster is called langouste and the fresh-water lobster is called écrevisse, so let's use the French terms here (without prejudice).

In culinary terms, langoustes are to all intents and purposes claw-less (non-chelate) lobsters.

Écrevisses have claws with microscopic amounts of rather delectable meat. The main edible part, the tail, contains about as much meat as a largish medium-sized prawn. Some people argue that écrevisse meat is better than prawn meat – it is certainly more expensive, except for those who can catch their own, or who live in particularly favoured areas. Louisiana recipes sometimes call for forty, sixty, or eighty écrevisses – millionaires' meals elsewhere.

Cream Sauce

Instant sophistication for deserving guests and deserving decapods. See WHITE WINE SAUCE for method.

Creole Shrimp

This is a lengthy but not a difficult recipe – and very worthwhile. It can be prepared in advance and is best made in large quantities. Use whole, uncooked prawns if possible, or uncooked headless, and if you want the authentic New Orleans appearance, devein them by loosening the intestine with a small sharp knife then pulling it away with finger and thumb.

> 3 lb whole or 2 lb headless medium to large prawns
> 3 onions, peeled and chopped
> 3 pimentos, red or yellow, seeded and chopped
> 3 sticks celery, chopped
> Vegetable oil
> 8 large TOMATOES, peeled and chopped
> 1 tsp cayenne pepper
> 1 tsp black pepper
> 1 tsp white pepper
> Basil
> Thyme
> Bay Leaf
> 2 tsps sugar

3 tsps salt
3 or more spring onions
Parsley

Peel the prawns and boil the heads and shells in 2 pints water for 20 minutes to make a rudimentary PRAWN STOCK. Strain it, discarding the shells.

For Creole sauce, which is the heart of this dish, you need a large, thick-bottomed but not very deep-sided pan. Slowly fry the onions, pimentos and celery in vegetable oil, stirring frequently. Let them get very soft but not brown or burnt. After about 40 minutes (*sic*), add the tomatoes, together with the cayenne, black and white peppers. Cook for a further 15 minutes, then add the prawn stock, basil, thyme, bay leaf, sugar and salt. Let this barely simmer for at least 2 hours, stirring occasionally and encouraging it with kindly glances.

At this stage the sauce can be put in the larder or fridge for use a day or two later, if required.

Shortly before you want to eat, reheat the sauce (if necessary), throw in the peeled (but still uncooked) prawns, and simmer them for 5-7 minutes. Finally, add the chopped spring onions and chopped parsley. Serve with rice.

Crevette
French word covering most shrimps and prawns. Very often it is qualified by a descriptive adjective – crevette grise, crevette nordique, and so on.

Crevettes à la Crème au Gratin
For 4 people as a starter:

1½ oz butter
¾ oz flour
Scant wineglass dry white wine or dry vermouth
2–3 tsps Dijon-type mustard
¼ pint double cream
Brandy
8 oz prawns, cooked and peeled
Breadcrumbs

Make a light ROUX with butter and flour, moisten it with wine or vermouth; stir in mustard. Make sure there are no lumps before adding cream and bringing the sauce to a leisurely boil. When it begins to thicken, add a few drops of brandy.

Put the prawns into a warm, fireproof dish and pour the creamy sauce over them. Sprinkle the top with breadcrumbs and strategically locate 2–3 small pieces butter among the crumbs. Grill for about 7 minutes.

Crevettes Frites

If ever you are offered ordinary shrimps which have not been cooked already, toss them in flour and deep-fry them in oil for 2 minutes. Then drain them, put them on a hot dish lined with absorbent paper and season with salt, paprika and lemon juice.

Crevettes au Paprika

BÉCHAMEL sauce
3 shallots, peeled and chopped finely
Butter
Paprika
1 lb prawns (peeled and cooked)

Prepare a generous ½ pint béchamel sauce using flour admixed with paprika in the ratio of 4 to 1. Alternatively, make a CREAM SAUCE which incorporates at least 1 tsp paprika.

Soften the shallots in butter. Add 2 tsps sweet paprika and mix well with the shallot. Add the prawns and stir so that each is coloured by the paprika. When they are heated through, fold them into the béchamel (or cream) sauce and serve with rice.

Curry Leaf

The leaf of *Murraya koenigii*; pungent and aromatic, it is widely used in Indian, especially south Indian, and Indonesian cooking. Bay leaf is not a substitute though it is something of a look-alike. Curry leaves can be bought in some Indian shops.

Dashi Powder —

— made from dried bonito flakes and kelp —

Dalna

Useful and mouth-filling Indian dish which stretches prawns with cabbage.

    2 onions, peeled
    3 cloves garlic
    2 fresh green chillies
    1 inch fresh ginger, peeled
    1 ½ tsps CORIANDER
    1 tsp cumin seeds
    1 medium Savoy or summer cabbage
    Vegetable oil
    8 oz cooked, peeled prawns (or uncooked, of course)
    3 cardamoms
    2 cloves
    1 inch cinnamon
    ½ pint yogurt
    1 tsp turmeric
    Salt
    1 tsp sugar

Mince one onion; slice the other. In a mortar or blender make a paste from the garlic, chillies, fresh ginger, coriander and cumin. Shred the cabbage.

Heat plenty of oil in a large, deep-sided pan and fry the prawns for 1 minute (longer if they are uncooked). Remove them and fry the sliced onion in same oil. When the onion is beginning to brown, add the spiced paste and minced onion. Fry for 5 minutes, then add the cabbage and stir-fry for 5 minutes, also adding cardamom, cloves and cinnamon.

Beat the yogurt briskly with turmeric and salt. Add it to the cabbage over medium heat, and cook for about 7 minutes, stirring frequently. Add sugar. When it is a good, appetising, unwatery consistency, stir in the prawns.

Serve with rice, dal and pappadums.

Dashi

This powder is the Nescafé of the FISH STOCK world. It can be bought from some oriental stores (especially Japanese specialists), also some health and whole-food shops. Failing dashi, there are a number of other fish-sauce products from the East which are helpful when you want instant fish stock. Or there is anchovy essence.

Dashi itself is made with bonito and seaweed.

Decapoda natantia
The great sub–order of crustacea to which all shrimps and prawns belong – literally, the ten-legged swimmers.

Decapoda reptantia
The other great sub–order of crustacea, the ten-legged crawlers – crabs and lobsters.

Deep-fried Prawns
For this Japanese (tempura) treatment, the prawns should be raw, shelled and headless, but have the tail fan intact.

Devein the prawns and score their undersides with a sharp knife. The underscoring operation prevents the prawns from curling when fried.

Either dip the prawns in the Japanese BATTER, or dust them with cornflour, brush them with white of egg and roll them in breadcrumbs.

Cut a green pimento into thin strips.

Heat oil in wok (or deep-fryer), and when it is almost smoking, fry the prawns, only a few at a time, for 2 minutes. Drain them on absorbent paper. When all the prawns are cooked, fry the uncooked pimento strips for 1 minute.

Serve prawns and pimento with a dip composed of soy sauce, sweetish sherry and either grated horseradish or grated fresh ginger. In Japan the sauce would also include a dash of – dashi.

Dehydration
Moisture loss affects the quality of prawns. It is a particular problem with frozen, peeled prawns, and the reason why these should be lightly glazed with water. Shells tend to keep the prawns moist without glazing. Severe moisture loss produces desiccation or freezer burn which ruins the prawn.

Over-hydration is another problem. Too much water either on the outside of a frozen prawn or within is sharp practice.

Determination of Sex
Biologists believe that prawns develop as males or females depending on the day length soon after they hatch. Those born early in the season, with more time to grow, usually become males. Those born later in the year have higher reproductive success if they develop as females. At Leeds University hatching larvae were divided into two groups. One group was kept in conditions which simulate the long days of summer;

the others were kept in chambers which simulated a short day length. The former tended to become males, the latter females. It is thought that long days activate the androgenic gland, which produces a hormone that causes testes to form.

Deveining

As described under ANATOMY, the vein or intestinal tract runs the full length of a prawn's tail from the back of its head. In some species, it is more obtrusive than others. Although harmless and, in most cases, tasteless, it can be unsightly. Both the Japanese and the Americans prefer deveined prawns or shrimp.

Removing the vein is easy enough, but time-consuming if a lot of prawns are involved. Use a small, sharp-pointed knife, or even a toothpick, to loosen it at the head end, then pull it away with finger and thumb.

With shrimps and small prawns deveining is unnecessary and much too fiddly. Peeled, frozen prawns tend to lose most of their veins in the processing.

Devilled Prawns

Dip shelled prawns (tail on, if possible) in melted butter. Toss them in a mixture of salt, black pepper and cayenne. Grill them for 2 minutes on each side. This is best with fairly large prawns – it makes a good savoury.

Alternatively mix together 1 tab French mustard, 1 tsp cayenne, 1 tsp black pepper, 1 tsp Worcestershire sauce, 1 tsp anchovy essence and the juice of 1 lemon. Stir this mixture into ½ pint double cream and mix well, adding for good measure a little salt and sugar.

This sauce can be used hot or cold. For the cold version, use only half the above quantity of mustard and whip the cream before introducing the devil. Then use the sauce with prawns or lobster (or crab) instead of mayonnaise.

For the hot version, pour the sauce over a dishful of prawns and place in hot oven or under the grill.

Devilled Shrimps Filippini

'Shell 1½ lb fresh-cooked shrimps, cut them in small pieces and place in a bowl; add 4 tabs breadcrumbs, ½ oz butter, the juice of a lemon, ½ tsp salt, ½ tsp French mustard, 1 tab Worcestershire sauce, 2 saltspoons cayenne, 2 beaten eggs, ¼ pint cream. Mix well and place whole in baking dish, sprinkle a little breadcrumbs over, then set in the oven for 15 minutes.'

A New York recipe by Filippini, formerly of Delmonico's.

Dill

Important culinary herb, *Anethum graveolens*, which is seriously compatible with prawns. It is much used in Scandinavian cooking and can be added beneficially to mayonnaise, sour cream, white sauces and salad dressings.

For a dill sauce to serve with hot prawns, make a ROUX with ½ oz butter and ½ oz flour. Add a small glass of sherry and a large glass of FISH or PRAWN STOCK, stirring to remove incipient lumps. Boil briskly and reduce by about one-third, before adding ¼ pint single cream or sour cream and 1½ tabs of finely chopped fresh dill. Bring to the boil and serve with poached (or heated through) prawns.

Aquavit or kümmel may be used instead of sherry.

Dominican Prawns

1 onion, peeled and chopped
1 lb okra (ladies' fingers), chopped
3 bananas (under-ripe if possible, or cooking bananas), peeled and
    sliced
2 TOMATOES, peeled and chopped
1 red chilli
4 tabs lemon juice
1 tab fresh CORIANDER leaf
1 lb shelled, deveined prawns

Fry the onion in oil until it is soft, then add the chopped okra. After 2 minutes, add banana, tomatoes, chilli, lemon juice and coriander leaf. Simmer about 5 minutes. Add prawns and cook another 5 minutes (less if using cooked prawns).

Serve dish with rice and drink a toast to the Dominican Republic.

Dublin Bay Prawn

Alias SCAMPO, alias langoustine, alias Norway lobster, alias *Nephrops norvegicus*.

Formerly spurned, now overrated (and overfished), with the plural of its Italian translation a *nom de guerre* to justify overpricing, this is one of the better decapods to eat but one of the worse to buy. In an experiment, I weighed 3 frozen, uncooked langoustines, thawed them slowly and weighed them again, cooked them and weighed the meat when extracted. From 7 oz whole uncooked weight, 2 oz of meat! At £6 per lb whole, uncooked weight, this means that langoustine meat (in this case, from Scotland) costs over £20 per pound. The weight loss was around 65 per cent, as opposed to whole lobster, where it is usually reckoned to average 50 per cent, whole prawns about 40 per cent, headless prawns about 20 per cent, or peeled prawns 5–10 per cent. And the much vaunted écrevisse has about the same meat to shell ratio as the langoustine.

So when looking at the apparent price of different decapods in a shop or market, it is as well to translate them into real prices by deducting the cost of the shell. You may then make a small adjustment in the shopkeeper's favour if you propose to use the head and shell for soup or sauce.

For my part, I am very happy to eat langoustines and écrevisses, am agnostic as to whether they are actually better than prawns or lobster, but am convinced that they are not so much better as to warrant such a whacking great premium price – double, or more than double, that of lobster.

And in Paris they are now selling langoustines so far below the age of consent that there is nothing to them at all.

Dumas on Shrimps

'There is no prettier sight than shrimps swimming in a bowl. The creatures themselves are transparent, like the glass enclosing them; and yet you see everything inside them, even the beating of the heart.

'It is usually women who fish for shrimps, pushing in front of them a net which scrapes along the sea-bed and collects everything to be found thereon.

'The shrimp lives for hardly two hours out of its element and needs to be cooked while still alive.

'The flesh of a live shrimp seems clammy, but after being cooked it is firm and beautifully white.

'The shrimps of the Channel coast are renowned, especially those from the vicinity of Le Havre, which bear the name bouquet. We invite tourists who are staying at Le Havre or Étretat to go and eat shrimps at St-Jour, at the establishment of the beautiful Ernestine. She is wise as well as beautiful, twenty-eight years old, owns a hotel and has a reputation which extends all along the coast. At her place you eat the finest shrimps which are fished for ten leagues around. It is the rendezvous for the gourmands of Le Havre, and for painters and poets from Paris, who have left respectively drawings and verses in her album in praise of her.'

Potage à la Crevette

'Take 6 fine tomatoes and 6 white onions and make a purée of them, half and half. Cook your shrimps in white wine with salt and pepper. Then peel the shrimps and put them aside on a plate, about 100 of them. Keep the bodies and boil them further with the seasoning used in cooking the shrimps, then pound them, bring them back to the boil, and pass them through a fine strainer.

'Now divide into 3 equal parts the excellent broth, the shrimp bisque and the purée of tomatoes and onions. Mix them together and bring them to the boil 3 or 4 times. Taste the mixture. If it has been well made and leaves nothing to be desired, throw in your shrimp tails and serve the soup boiling hot.'

From Alan and Jane Davidson's translation, *Dumas on Food*.

According to my reading of this recipe, 'the excellent broth' and the shrimp bisque are already combined at the stage that Dumas tells us to mix them together.

E

Eggplant and prawn Casserole —
a recipe from Maine USA

Écrevisse

The fresh-water, lobster-like crayfish – *Astacus astacus*. They are usually about half the size of a small lobster, but can grow very large. In his fascinating book, *Crustaceans*, Waldo Schmitt reports a Tasmanian specimen weighing 9 lb.

Like so many things, écrevisses were plentiful and cheap in the bad old days. Greek slaves used to eat them, according to Pliny, rather as the Victorian lower orders lived on oysters and salmon. Écrevisses have all but disappeared from most of the rivers and lakes of western Europe, including the British Isles. The famous restaurants of France now have to make do with écrevisses imported from places like Poland and Turkey.

It is not over-eating or over-fishing which is to blame, but the fungal plague, *Aphanomyces astaci*, which first struck in Italy in 1860, and slowly but surely spread across Europe. It reached Sweden's Lake Hjalmaren in 1908, devastating the famous écrevisse population, which used to yield five million specimens a year. Since when – *ingeting*. The deadly fungus was not found in England until 1981. It is doubtful if the native species will survive.

However, écrevisse farming of the plague-resistant signal crayfish from North America is beginning to take off, and Britain now has a crayfish marketing organisation located in Gillingham, Dorset. It will be interesting to see whether this increases the supply and therefore reduces the cost of these decapods, or whether it merely erodes the pensions of retired colonels.

The Swedes are excessively fond of *Astacus astacus*, which they call *krefta*, and have a special *kreftafest* every year in August. One of the best places for this feast is Strindberg's Red Room.

Canada seems to be a good place for wild écrevisses. A few years ago, my elder son caught about 50 one afternoon on a small lake north of Toronto, and very good they were too.

Eggplant and Shrimp Casserole

1 large onion, peeled and chopped
1 large green pimento, seeded and chopped
Butter
2 eggplants (aubergines), peeled and chopped
1 clove garlic, peeled
1 lb TOMATOES, peeled and chopped
Parsley
Salt and pepper

Breadcrumbs
1 lb cooked shrimp

A recipe from Maine. Fry the onion and pimento in butter. In a little butter and water, separately cook the eggplants and garlic to a pulp. Add tomatoes, chopped and peeled (canned will do), and cook till the mixture is thick; add parsley and the onion mixture. Simmer for 5 minutes. Season with salt and pepper.

Mix breadcrumbs with softened butter and parsley. Butter a casserole and layer it with the eggplant mixture, shrimp and crumbs alternately, finishing with the crumbs. Bake in a hot oven for about 15 minutes.

Eggs

Female prawns produce very large quantities of tiny eggs. I have heard estimates ranging from 200,000 to two million per spawning but am too innumerate to assess their credibility. Unlike lobster coral or caviar, prawn eggs are not very nice to eat.

Eggs and Shrimps

Another Dumas recipe. 'Take 12 eggs and break them into a salad bowl, using all the yolks, but only 8 of the whites. If there is too much egg white, it detracts from the delicacy of the dish.

'In a separate pan boil the bodies (minus the tails, which you reserve) of the shrimps, adding a glass of Chablis wine. Have it all bubble up 2 or 3 times, then pour everything into a mortar to make a purée of it. This you then press through a fine sieve, to remove even the smallest bits of carapace.

'Blend this fine purée with the eggs, to which you have already added salt and pepper, and which you have lightly decorated with finely chopped spring onions and parsley. Next add to this the peeled shrimp tails, beat them up with the eggs and pour everything into a frying pan which has been buttered with good fresh butter. Cook and turn out carefully on a platter.'

From Alan and Jane Davidson's translation, *Dumas on Food*.

See also BOILED EGGS.

English Butter Sauce

An old-fashioned sauce which goes excellently with all crustaceans, and can be spiked with anchovy, sherry, fennel and other influences.

Put 3 oz unsalted butter in a pan with pepper and grated nutmeg. Add 1 oz sifted flour when the butter melts, kneading the whole with a wooden spoon. Add ½ pint cold water, stir this in, heating the sauce till it boils. Let it simmer for 20 minutes without allowing it to become too thick, then whip in 6 oz of butter, teaspoon by teaspoon, stirring and whipping as you do so. At this point, the pan should stand over very gentle heat or in a bain-marie. If the whipped butter begins to oil, add a spoonful of cold water, then another if necessary. Finish with a few drops of lemon juice and salt to your taste.

If the sauce has to wait, stand the pan in a vessel of hot water. It will spoil if too hot. Francatelli's recipe, in his book, *The Modern Cook*.

Etouffée

2 lb unshelled prawns (uncooked if possible)
2 large crabs
2 large onions, peeled and chopped finely
4 stalks celery, chopped finely
2 red or yellow pimentos, seeded and chopped finely
2 oz flour
3 tabs vegetable oil
Salt
1 tsp cayenne
1 tsp ground black pepper
1 tsp ground white pepper
1 cup chopped parsley
6 spring onions

Peel the prawns. Remove all meat from the crab. Pound up the crab shells and use them, with the prawn shells, to make 2 pints of crab and PRAWN STOCK.

At the same time, fry the onions, celery and pimento until they are more or less caramelised – about 30 minutes. Also prepare a brown roux with the flour and vegetable oil instead of butter.

When the onion mixture is soft and brown, stir the roux into it; add salt, red pepper, black pepper and white pepper; then add (slowly) the strained crab and prawn stock, stirring with a wooden spoon to eliminate lump formation. Simmer the mixture for 30 minutes. (These New Orleans recipes need long, slow cooking.)

Add the prawns, if they are uncooked, and after about 6 minutes add the crab meat, assuming it is cooked. Finally, stir in the parsley and the chopped spring onions.

Euphasia superba

The Antarctic KRILL.

Exhippolysmata ensirostris

Small, shallow-water shrimp caught mainly off the Indian coast and points east. Important locally rather than internationally.

Eyesight

Although it sometimes seems that prawns have their eyes out on stalks, their eyesight is usually poor. They make up for this by very acute sensory devices such as the hairs they have on most of their appendages, and their antennae. (My brother-in-law, who became a reluctant vegetarian some years ago, has relented to the extent of eating mussels, oysters and other bivalves on the ground that they have no eyes. I am hoping that in time he will add creatures with weak eyesight to his dispensations.)

See ZOOLOGISTS AT NIGHT.

F

Audbjørg

— fishing the fjordurs

Factories and Freezing

Prawn factories under the Arctic Circle are pretty much like prawn factories on the equator. The main difference is that up north the pace of life is relaxed and leisurely, while in the tropics it is urgent and thrusting – time is of the essence; an interesting reversal of normal perceptions.

In Ecuador (or Indonesia) the prawns must be frozen within hours of being extracted from sea or pond. Unless they reach the factory very quickly, they will be useless. The aim is to have them in the freezer within six to twelve hours, though if ice is plentiful, they can last a full day. In Iceland they reckon that the third day is the earliest prawns should be processed, the fourth is the best and the fifth perfectly all right. It's all a question of weather. Ecuador's ambient temperature of some 85°F is great for growing large, plump prawns but perilous for processing them; the North Atlantic seabed's 35°F means a spartan life, slow growth, under-achievement in size – seldom more than three inches, often less – but after their capture, the outside environment for two-thirds of the year is almost a refrigeration process in its own right. Thus nature helps and hinders impartially between the two areas – one gains on the swings while the other gains on the roundabouts.

The main processes are grading by size, washing, freezing and packing. In Ecuador and other points tropical, the heads are often removed from the raw prawns but the shells left intact. In Iceland, Norway and Greenland the prawns are usually cooked and very often peeled. Cooking is done by steam and takes ninety seconds to two minutes. Shelling follows, though the larger ones may be left unshelled. Machine shelling is wasteful since it yields only half as much meat as hand shelling.

Peeled North Atlantic prawns undergo two further processes: first, they are bathed in BRINE to restore the salinity they have lost in the cooking and peeling; second, they are sprayed with fresh water immediately after being frozen so that each has a thin glaze of ice to protect it from freezer burn and preserve its moisture content.

At a factory I visited in northern Iceland, there is yet another process. Twice a day, work stops and the girls, who have been bending over conveyor belts to grade and assess the prawns, do physical exercises to music, for the benefit of backs and torsos. On my visit the music was 'Daisy, Daisy, give me your answer do'.

Feta Prawn Puffs

    1 onion, chopped
    3 tabs olive oil

2 cloves garlic, chopped
14 oz can TOMATOES
⅓ pint dry white wine
Salt and pepper
6 oz feta cheese, crumbled
4 oz cooked, shelled prawns, chopped
2 spring onions, finely chopped
4 tabs yogurt (Greek if possible)
1 tsp fresh oregano (or marjoram or basil)
14 oz puff pastry
Flour for dusting
1 egg, beaten (to glaze pastry)
6 green olives, stoned and sliced
Parsley, (flat-leaved if possible)
Lemon juice (optional)

First make a tomato and olive sauce: melt onion in olive oil, add garlic, and when garlic is soft, add tomatoes, wine, salt and pepper. Cook gently for about 20 minutes, till sauce is thick and homogeneous.

Mix the cheese and prawns with the spring onions and yogurt; flavour with pepper and the chosen herb.

Roll out the pastry and cut 16 rounds about 4 ins in circumference. Place 8 rounds on dampened baking tray(s), and spoon cheese filling into the centre of each. Brush the edges with egg, and top with the remaining rounds, sealing the edges. Make a small slit in the top of each parcel with a knife. Brush with beaten egg and bake in a medium to hot oven 400°F, Gas Mark 6 for 15–20 minutes, till puffs are puffed and golden.

Finish the sauce with chopped olives and parsley, re-heating it if necessary. The sauce may also be sharpened with lemon juice. Serve the sauce with the puffs. Acknowledgment: *Taste* magazine.

Fish Fumet
See FISH STOCK.

Fish Soup
This is a sturdy northern soup, tasting of the Irish Sea rather than the Mediterranean.

1 lb unshelled prawns or shrimps
1 lb hake, haddock, cod or whiting, cut into pieces
1 onion

1 carrot
1 stick celery
2 TOMATOES
Dried mixed herbs
Dry cider
Soft breadcrumbs
Cream (optional entirely)
Parsley or dill

Peel the prawns and put their heads and shells into a large saucepan with the white fish, the roughly chopped vegetables, the dried herbs, a glass of cider and 2½ pints water. Bring to the boil and simmer for about 25 minutes. The white fish should virtually disintegrate.

Pound the peeled prawns with roughly the same quantity of soft breadcrumbs.

Pass the FISH STOCK through a fine strainer, squeezing the debris with the back of a spoon.

Put the prawn mixture into the saucepan and add the fish broth little by little, at first making a paste, then diluting it. Season with salt and pepper. Simmer for 2–3 minutes.

This soup is excellent without cream, slightly more luxurious with. It is even more luxurious if the cream is mixed with 2–3 egg yolks (so long as care is taken not to boil it once the egg has been incorporated). With or without these additions, a generous hand with parsley or dill at the last minute is mandatory.

Fish Stock

A great many prawn dishes are significantly improved by the use of a good fish stock. There are many recipes for fish stock, some simple, some elaborate. Most of them carry the disadvantage that the smell of boiling fish is unappetising. One general rule is that if heads and bones are included, the boiling time should be restricted to not more than half an hour, preferably 20–25 minutes. Overcooking produces fish glue instead of fish stock.

For a simple version add fish bones, heads, trimmings, and if you can spare it a little fish too, to a COURT BOUILLON. Simmer for 25 minutes, then strain off the broth. After that the stock can be concentrated by fast boiling without producing glue.

Alternatively, a court bouillon in which fish has been poached can be kept and used as fish stock.

Prawn heads and shells are, of course, a very appropriate addition to any fish stock which is destined to participate in a sauce for a prawn dish. Indeed, they make a serviceable stock without any other fish, only a little carrot and shallot.

Oily fish such as mackerel and herring are usually omitted from fish-stock mixtures. A bay leaf is often included.

As mentioned under DASHI, there are oriental sauces and pastes which can be used as instant fish stock in an emergency. So can canned fish soup of various kinds – depending on what the stock is going to be used for – or even turtle soup.

Fishing at the Seaside

'Prawns are a source of pure joy. Shrimps, in the appreciation of which gourmet and tyro speak with one voice, are justly considered even more delicate. Not only used their pursuit to keep the children happily occupied, the existence of the shrimp was shrouded in another and higher purpose. Even in mid-Victorian days Mildred, still "no more than a child", yet undoubtedly nubile, armed with a shrimping net, was tacitly allowed to show, bared and rosy, the major part of those graceful legs which the Almighty had given her for some inscrutable but disturbing reason ("extremities" the existence of which might otherwise never have been suspected), without any fear of censure.'

From P. Morton Shand, *A Book of Food*. Mr Shand's daughter is now Lady Howe, wife of Sir Geoffrey. Her name is Elspeth.

Fishing the Fjordurs

Hvammstangi, northern Iceland, 8 April 1989

0600 Arrive at harbour and board 20-ton trawler *Audbjorg*. Temperature −5°C.

0605 Tea in cabin with Gunnar-Thor Gunnarsson, the Captain's son, only English-speaking member of 3-man crew. Cabin snug (+25°C) – table, lockers, just slept-in bunks, galley with cauldron simmering.

0610 One of the bunks comes to life – Benni gets out, puts on his boots without a word, goes on deck.

0615 Steaming out of Hvammstangi.

0630 Net goes out for first time. 10 minutes to get it down to seabed. Soon trawling at 50 fathoms; boat steaming dead slow.

0700 More tea. Gunnar-Thor (G-T) despondent about poor catch yesterday (1 tonne). Benni eats sweets. Captain at helm.

0730   G-T takes a nap. Write notes and try to think up sensible questions.

0800   Feeling sleepy after early start. G-T sees me nodding off, suggests I help myself to a bunk. Do so, but immediately stop feeling sleepy.

0815   News on radio translated by G-T as US nuclear submarine explodes in Norwegian waters.

0845   All hands on deck for day's first trawl.

0900   Catch deposited in deep, 8ft × 6ft wooden box on deck. Catch poor, so skipper decides to go elsewhere. Full steam ahead while G-T and Benni start sorting and boxing. At least 95 per cent prawns but also sild and other unwanted species, including marhnutur which must be thrown back into sea. Offer to help, am given rubber gloves and waterproof overall. Prawns loaded into plastic boxes holding 40 kg. Sort takes 30 minutes. Fat seagulls feast on sild we throw away, but the marhnutur, after a moment of stunned adjustment to their escape, wiggle gratefully down towards the bottom.

0945   G-T suggests I try a live prawn. Throwing inhibition to mercifully mild breeze (temp now about 0°C), I do so. Delicious.

0946   Eat two more live prawns. Trawling starts in different part of fjordur.

0955   Sample dried (unsalted) haddock in cabin. Papery texture, not much taste, but nicer than dried salt cod. Benni eating chocolate thoughtfully.

1000   News that nuclear sub was Russian not American.

1005   G-T says person he most admires is Mrs Thatcher.

1020   Iceland has one part per million of world population, yet has 50 percent of its most beautiful women – 2 out of the last 4 Miss Worlds being Icelandic. We discuss the odds against this, and the implications. (Benni eating Polar mints.)

1040   Sorting second catch – worse than first. Snowing. Skipper sets westerly course for opposite fjordur. Boat rolls a great deal. (How Juliet would hate us throwing away so much fish – some of them look like baby soles, others like mini sardines.)

1120   Next trawl begins.

1135 Disturbing news: no lav on board. Resolve to eat and drink as little as possible, and pray for temporary constipation.

1150 Stops snowing; foggy sunshine.

1200 News that 18 of Soviet crew are dead.

1210 Manage to sneak a pee over (leeward) side with no one looking except gulls – skipper at helm, G-T asleep again, Benni eating jelly babies.

1245 Real sunshine. Find niche on deck and bask.

1330 Seems a long trawl. Sun clouds over. Go below to find G-T and Benni watching teach-yourself German programme on TV (black and white and fuzzy).

1350 Skipper a man of few words – handsome, serious, sandy-bearded Viking. When I give him a bottle of Irish whiskey, he almost smiles and grips my hand by way of thanks. Then I put bottle in his unmade bunk.

1400 TV switches to sport. Mostly football. Words like Liverpool, Sheffield Wednesday and Chelsea all part of the Icelandic vocabulary. Cautiously accept half mug of coffee and small cheese sandwich.

1410 Third catch coming up at last. Larger than the other two put together. And surely less waste? Secretly put aside some of the despised disposables as we sort, meaning to create a sort of Babette's Feast and give my hosts a fish tea. Baudroie aux queues de crevettes (some of them look like angler fish)? Wonder if there's any dill. Am soon caught in the act by G-T. Next trawl continues in same area as we sort.

1500 All boxed. In galley G-T finds committedly anti-non-stick frying pan and cooking, of a kind, takes place. Sole-like fish prove under-privileged dabs; sardine analogues made of cottonwool, but the ugly angler beast, which turns out to be a mini monkfish, is good, and the prawns, cooked à la plancha on salt, are outstanding. The skipper joins us; Benni prefers the Icelandic equivalent of wine gums.

1545 Benni decides to show how cooking should be done. He throws 3 frankfurters on the hotplate. One catches light almost immediately, the others produce smoke without fire. Then he washes them under the tap, wipes them, and throws them back on the hotplate with much the same result. Process repeated a third time, then the sausages dipped into a wide-necked ketchup bottle and consumed in a trice. Their aroma scents the afternoon watch as we hear that Liverpool beat Sheffield Wednesday 5–1.

1610   Imprudently accept a can of non-alcoholic lager bearing the respectable and prophylactic brand name Sanitas.

1645   Fourth haul coming up (watched by seal). The big one. Takes 2 hours to sort, and has more fiddly sild than before – silver needles in a pink pin cushion. Right hand and both feet gradually register falling temperature, rising wind: back protests at constant bending to extricate fish from deep box. Gulls feast but show no thanks. The more we give the more they want.

1840   Finished at last. G-T tots up the boxes – 33, over 1.3 tonnes. But our 12-hour day must be ending. All too soon it's bath time, vodka time, supper time? Not at all, G-T assures me. We have been trawling the whole of the last 2 hours, going back on our tracks among these rich pickings; with any luck the next trawl will be even bigger and take 3 hours. And we should still have time for another on the way back to Hvammstangi. My relief palpable as I do my sums. But the failing light? No problem, we have a very strong masthead lamp.

1850   No wonder Gunnar-Thor is a Thatcherite. They have had catches 3 times as big, that's what he likes. (Or is it that Mrs T is actually a Gunnar-Thorite?) He lends me an extra pair of socks.

1900   Football has given way to snooker on TV. Young Icelanders mimick Steve Davis, handle the chalk very professionally, and solemnly fail to pot balls. At same time radio informs us that 60 Soviet sailors are dead and Norway is very cross with Russia.

1915   All – even Benni – sit down to stew of salt mutton, potatoes and swedes. Could have been improved by onions, but otherwise masterly, specially the swedes. Skipper brewed it without any fuss whatever. TV now has nauseating film of showbiz self-congratulation called *Fame*, but the Icelandic subtitles are nice.

1945   Fifth catch. Not as large as fourth. Pity. But larger than all the others. Very muddy and needs constant slooshing with buckets of sea-water. Severe test for loyal moonboots, which have always been impenetrable to Alpine snows but now acknowledge defeat, joining back, hands, arms, etc., among the wets. Catch a veritable mine of sild – bonanza for the gulls. Shall relish the next gulls' eggs which come my way.

2110   Second pee – in the gloaming (but to windward). All OK in other department.

2115   A few minutes of *The Three Musketeers* on TV – spoof version which got panned a few years ago, but the duelling on ice funny. G-T lends me 2 more pairs of real Icelandic wool socks and gives me 2 plastic bags. I put the bags over the socks and into the wet moonboots. Works a treat.

2120   Last haul, and a doddle – as virginally clean as the previous was sullied. All except mud destined for Marks & Spencer. We finish sorting in under the hour by floodlight. Haul includes 5 starfish, 2 lumpfish, a skate and what looked like a small salmon. G-T keeps the lumpfish.

2215   Chugging peacefully homewards with 3.6 tonnes of prawns and a little adhering mud. The Musketeers are thwarting Richelieu and Milady; Thatcher's protegé has earned £360 in 18 hours; Benni's earnings should enable him to patronise the local sweetshops without financial worry. The skipper's cup is full too – he has a bottle of John Jameson (but hasn't opened it yet – no Exxon captain he).

2245   Landfall in harbour just as truck arrives to collect catch. Loading it will take another 50 minutes. Having seen that routine last night, I leave it to the experts, and plod up the hill in my plastic bags. The bar is still open and purveys Icelandic aquavit with a smile.

Food Poisoning
See WARNING SIGNS.

Food Values
Prawns are a nutritious, high protein foodstuff, low in fat. Such fat as they do have – about 1 per cent of shelled body weight – is predominantly polyunsaturated. They contain significant quantities of calcium and phosphorus, essential trace elements, and of the amino-3 fatty acids, which are thought to reduce the risk of heart attacks. The average calorie count of prawns is 90–100 per 3½ oz portion.

Fresh Prawns
Prawns deteriorate much faster than most other fish, but remain good for two or three days if kept on ice. In theory it is possible for prawns caught off Greenland or Malaysia on Monday morning to be on sale in London by Tuesday lunchtime, and for them still to be sweet and safe

on Wednesday afternoon, even Thursday, if they have been nurtured responsibly all the time. There are shops in London's Chinatown where you can buy such prawns, but somehow I never want to. They do not carry a Best Before label and usually look a bit woebegone. Yet fresh, unfrozen prawns are obtainable in most cities which take their seafood seriously – New York, Madrid, Paris. While the potential supply of unfrozen prawns may well increase as transportation becomes ever faster, and relatively cheaper, it will require a positive revolution to bring them within easy reach of the average supermarket shopper.

At the top end of the market there is an embryonic trade in live shrimp. It has been found that certain species can be flown across the world live if packed in chilled seaweed. This is not a cheap process, and needless to say the principal market is Japan, where enthusiasm for shrimp knows no bounds.

Incidentally, there is a growing international trade in live lobster. In 1988 lobsters from Maine and eastern Canada, flown live from Boston, could be bought in London for £5 per lb.

Fresh-water Prawns

The giant river prawn (MACROBRACHIUM ROSENBERGII), native to brackish estuaries around the Indian Ocean, is extremely fine eating, and is one of the largest commercial prawns, reaching over a foot in length. It is also one of the species which is being farmed successfully in many parts of the tropics, and one which is exported live (in very small quantities).

Fresh-water prawns can be bought in England and are well worth seeking out. The usual commercial form is frozen, shell on, head off, uncooked – and the ratio of meat to shell is very high – about 80:20. Uncooked, they are a dingy bluey-greeny-grey, but they turn an attractive pinky-red almost as soon as they come into contact with cooking temperatures.

A related species, the painted river prawn (*Macrobrachium carcinus*) is indigenous from Florida to Brazil. It is usually not quite as large as its oriental cousin, but reaches a good 9 inches if not fished out of its habitat too soon. A 3 lb specimen, whose body length was 10½ inches and feelers 26½ inches, was caught in the Devil's River, Texas.

Macrobrachium carcinus is being farmed, too, although as yet not on a scale which makes it a regular export item.

Fricassée de Crevettes
    1½ lb unshelled prawns
    3 shallots, peeled and chopped

2 carrots, peeled and chopped
1 stick celery, chopped
Butter
Brandy
¼ pint sweet white wine
¼ pint single cream (or more)
Tarragon or chervil
Salt
White pepper
Tabasco

Remove the heads and shells from the prawns (uncooked if possible).

Soften the shallot, carrot and celery in butter. Add the shells and heads and fry them for 3 minutes. Then flare them with 1 tab warm brandy. Then add sweet white wine and an equal quantity of water. Simmer the shells and vegetables for 10 minutes before adding the cream. Simmer a further 3 minutes. Then strain the sauce through a fine sieve into another pan, squeezing as much as possible out of the shells, and so on. Throw away the sieved debris.

Add the chervil or tarragon, then the prawns, to the sauce and cook for as long as the prawns require – about 7 minutes if they are raw, 2 minutes if cooked. Season with salt, pepper and a shot of tabasco.

Transfer to a serving dish and sprinkle the top with a little more chervil or tarragon. Serve with boiled rice.

Fried Prawns

All prawnivorous nations have their own ways of frying prawns and shrimp. Many of the other recipes in this book, for example GAMBAS AJILLO, could appear under this heading. The simplest way is to toss cooked, shelled prawn in oil or butter with salt and pepper, perhaps finishing them with parsley and lemon. This is very good, and it works equally well with uncooked, unshelled prawns if the cooking time is extended three or four minutes or longer, of course, for very large specimens. Here are two other versions, one European, one Indian.

2 cloves garlic, chopped finely
Fresh tarragon, basil or oregano, chopped finely
Olive oil
Butter
¼ tsp black pepper
1 lb prawns, uncooked if possible
Lemon juice

Marinate the prawns for at least half an hour in olive oil and lemon juice.

Heat a little olive oil and butter and fry the garlic for 2 minutes without letting it brown. Add black pepper, and stir it into the garlic. Then add the prawns. Cook them for 4–5 minutes, according to size. After 3 minutes throw in most of the chopped herbs.

Serve the prawns with all their butter and oil, sprinkling the remaining herbs and a little more lemon juice on top. If you eat them with your fingers, you will need napkins and finger bowls.

The Indian version of fried prawns calls for:

1 coconut or 3 tabs desiccated coconut
1 lb prawns, uncooked if possible
1 tsp turmeric
1 tsp cayenne
CURRY LEAVES or CORIANDER LEAVES
Vegetable oil or ghee
1 onion, peeled and sliced

Put the grated or desiccated coconut into a saucepan and mix in the prawns, turmeric, cayenne and coriander or curry leaf. Add just enough hot water for a short boiling operation, about 5 minutes, at the end of which the mixture should be reasonably dry.

Heat oil or ghee, and fry the onion until it is brown. Add the prawn and coconut mixture, and stir-fry until it is a golden brown and red.

Fritto Misto Mare

Italian fish and chips without the chips. The secret is to use good olive oil, or at the very least a mixture of olive oil and a light vegetable oil such as sunflower. A minimum of three kinds of fish should be included, for contrast of taste and texture – prawns, squid and red mullet are traditional, but fillets of cod, plaice, sole or catfish (rock salmon) can be used instead of red mullet. The fish and the squid should be cut into pieces slightly larger and slightly smaller respectively than the prawns.

The ingredients can either be dipped in a light flour and water (1 oz flour to 5 tabs water) BATTER or be dusted with flour before being fried. The prawns may either be peeled and decapitated with tail fan intact, or whole, unpeeled: Better still, have a selection of both forms. The unpeeled prawns should not be embattered.

It is not necessary to use a deep fryer. A fairly capacious frying pan or a wok is recommended, with a generous supply of oil. The oil must be very hot. Fry the fish in small batches, transferring them, when crisp and golden, to a hot dish (via absorbent paper). Fry the unpeeled prawns last.

Serve the fritto misto mare with plenty of lemon wedges and a sprinkling of parsley. French bread is a good accompaniment. Some people recommend tartare sauce or aïoli.

Frozen Prawns

As pointed out in the Introduction, this is by far the most common commercial form of prawn. The industry reckons that at least 90 per cent of the world's commercial catch, including farmed prawns, is now frozen. Gastronomically that is perhaps a pity, but not a disaster. Freezing technology has come a long way since Elizabeth David declared that frozen scampi were not worth eating. When frozen in good condition and under good conditions, and defrosted slowly, ideally in a refrigerator, the resulting seafood is nearly as good as freshly caught and immediately cooked prawns, and perhaps better than 'fresh' prawns which, after two days on ice in a boat, have slithered their way through various chilly wholesale stages finally to end up on a retail slab. This is not to say that the trade, which knows quite well how swiftly prawns go off, is irresponsible. Prawns of unmarketable quality are rare, as is shellfish poisoning.

Yet processing under ideal conditions cannot be guaranteed and no doubt the acknowledged poor quality of some of the warm-water prawns on sale in England is due to less than perfect conditions in their country of origin.

There must also be reservations about the increasing practice of freezing prawns on the trawler as they are caught, de-freezing them later on shore, and re-freezing them after peeling and cooking. The process seems perfectly safe, but the prawns lose some of their taste and texture by the time they are re-thawed. When all is said and done, they have become convenience foods.

The cooked, peeled, frozen prawn is an attractive and useful product. The unpeeled cooked prawn is better eating. The uncooked, unpeeled prawn is the least convenient form, but the most rewarding and versatile in the kitchen. It is to be hoped that the prawn industry will soon make it as easy to buy uncooked prawns in the United Kingdom as it is in France, Spain and the United States.

G

Ginger

Garlic

highly compatible to prawns

Gambas Ajillo

One of the most popular tapas in Spanish bars.

> Unshelled prawns
> Olive oil
> Garlic, chopped coarsely
> Chillies (fresh or dried), chopped coarsely

Heat the olive oil in a heavy frying pan or fireproof earthenware dish (cazuela de barro). Add at least 1 clove garlic and 1 chilli, more if you want extra pungency. Without letting these ingredients burn or even discolour significantly, let the oil take up their flavours by cooking them gently for several minutes. To fry the prawns, increase the heat, and allow them about 1 minute on each side, before removing the pan and allowing them to continue cooking in the retained heat for 2–3 minutes.

Serve the prawns with at least some of their cooking oil, plenty of salt, bread for dipping into the oil and beer or very dry sherry.

Gambas a la Plancha

A la plancha cooking (literally 'on the plate') in practice means toasting on a hotplate or griddle with hardly any oil or fat. The prawns should, however, be brushed with a mixture of oil and lemon juice twice or thrice during the toasting process. Crushed garlic is sometimes added to the basting mixture, and a good deal of crunchy sea salt is scattered on prawns and hotplate.

Traditionally, live prawns were used for this dish. As with GAMBAS AJILLO, the finished product should be eaten with the fingers and with friends.

Gamberi in Umido

One of Italy's favourite ways of cooking scampi, this works equally well with good-sized DECAPODA NATANTIA.

> 1 lb shelled, uncooked prawns
> 3 tabs olive oil
> 1 clove garlic, peeled and chopped
> Juice of 1 lemon
> 3 tabs chopped parsley
> 1 tab capers

Stew the prawns gently in olive oil for 5 minutes. Then add garlic, lemon juice, parsley and capers. Cover the pan and stew for a further 5 minutes, stirring once or twice.

Serve the prawns with the lemon and oil in which they were cooked.

Garlic

Sulphur compounds are responsible for the pungency of garlic and the rest of the allium family. When these ingredients are crushed or chopped, enzymes convert sulphur-containing (and nitrogen-containing) amino acids into volatile materials which seem to be positive and powerful aromas but which are actually smelly disulphides. Enzyme action on amino acids in onions may also make you cry, but I have forgotten the name of the lachrymatory chemical which is responsible. Whatever the chemistry, and however red the eyes, garlic and prawns remain highly compatible.

Garlic Prawns

An American version of Spain's GAMBAS AJILLO.

> 1 lb peeled prawns
> 6 cloves garlic, peeled
> Parsley
> Olive oil

Chop the parsley and crush 4 of the garlic cloves. Mix these together in a pudding bowl and add the prawns. Stir to make sure that each prawn is exposed to the parsley and garlic mixture. Leave them (covered with clingfilm) to soak up their environment for several hours if possible, and if the weather is hot put them in a refrigerator.

To cook: chop the remaining garlic and cook it, not too quickly, in olive oil. When it is beginning to turn golden, add the prawn and parsley mixture. Fry over medium heat for 2–7 minutes, depending on whether you are using cooked or uncooked prawns.

Ghee

Clarified butter as used for frying in Indian cooking, especially north Indian. Its advantage is that, lacking the water and milk solids content of ordinary butter, it can be heated to very high temperatures without burning. A possible disadvantage is that, according to some medical reports, ghee users are somewhat more prone to heart disease than people who use oil or unclarified butter. If this is true, it reverses the previous view that ghee is healthier than ordinary butter.

The special taste of Indian clarified butter comes from the very slow clarification process and the use of butter made from well soured milk, often buffaloes'.

To clarify shop butter, heat it slowly and note that the milk solids either rise to the top or sink to the bottom. Skim the solids off the top, then pour off the melted butter in the middle, leaving the remaining solids in the pan. The solids need not be thrown away. They can be used deliciously to baste prawns and other fish for grills and barbecues.

Ginger

One of the spices which has a particularly strong affinity for prawns, ginger is used in innumerable Asiatic recipes.

Zinghiber officinale, of which the root or rhizome provides the cooking spice, is indigenous to southern Asia. For export to colder climes, its tuberous roots have been dried and powdered, or crystallised, or preserved in syrup (Chinese ginger), for centuries. For some years, however, they have also been sent to Europe in their unprocessed root form, and they can now be bought not only in specialist oriental outlets, but in department stores, health food shops and the larger supermarkets. Although they wither and dry out eventually, they have quite a long larder shelf life – about 3 weeks, depending on their condition when bought. A tip from Madhur Jaffrey: if you fill a flowerpot with sandy soil and press the ginger partly into it, it will not only stay fresh but grow, as long as it is watered occasionally.

For most culinary purposes, fresh root ginger is much better than the other forms. Powdered ginger gives melon a mildly addictive tickle, and Chinese ginger still makes a good Christmas present.

In Asiatic cooking, ginger is often used in conjunction with several other spices – it is an ingredient of many curries and curry powders, for example. The recipe which follows is for those who like their ginger less adulterated.

Gingered Prawns

1 tab fresh ginger, peeled and finely chopped
1 clove garlic, chopped
1½ tsps coarsely ground black pepper
Butter
1 lb prawns
Large wine glass ginger wine
Juice of 1 lemon
Salt

Fry ginger, garlic and black pepper in butter gently for 10 minutes. Add the prawns and stir them around. After 2 minutes (5 for uncooked prawns) add the ginger wine (Crabbie's if possible) and turn up the heat. Let the wine bubble for 30 seconds, then put a lighted match to it and obtain a mini ignition. Shake the pan vigorously. When the flame dies, add the lemon juice and a little salt.

This makes a piquant first course. Increase the black pepper content (crushed in a mortar rather than ground in a mill) and it provides a palate-stimulating savoury; equally it serves very well as one of several dishes in an Indian or Indonesian-type meal, along with rice, a fish or chicken curry and some spiced vegetable dishes.

Very good made with green peppercorns instead of black.

Ginny Prawns

Simple and slightly sinful, this can be an impressive main course with *Macrobrachium rosenbergii* or *Penaeus monodon*, but also makes a diverting starter, as in the quantities indicated below, with smaller species.

    1 small shallot per person, peeled and chopped finely
    ½ oz butter per person
    Cayenne
    2 oz peeled, cooked prawns per person
    1 tab gin per person
    2 tabs cream per person
    Lemon juice
    Salt

Gently fry the shallots in the butter, with a shot of cayenne or tabasco. Add the prawns. Toss them about in the butter, and when there is no doubt that they are hot right through, flare them with the warmed gin. Gin, incidentally, seems to burn longer than brandy. When the flame at last dies, add the cream and, stirring the while, cook it quite fast for 2 minutes. Before serving, sharpen with lemon juice and season with salt.

Glaze

In the seafood industry, this means the protective coating of ice on a frozen product. The coating is altogether necessary, for without it freezer burn and DEHYDRATION will ruin the prawn. However, by incorporating more water than is necessary, for example by spraying and freezing the prawns over and over again, unscrupulous packers can abuse the system. There have been cases where '1 lb' packs have proved, on being thawed, to be over 50 per cent water by weight. Effective regulations prevent this in some markets, including the United States. In the United Kingdom, prawn packers are becoming increasingly committed to self-policing, and most reputable firms label their packs with both the gross weight and the weight net of water, that is the thawed weight. The latter shows the true cost of the contents. But bear in mind that prawns, like all crustaceans, indeed all fish, contain a fair amount of water naturally in their cells. Some of this natural moisture can be lost it they are defrosted quickly or by microwave, since rapid thawing breaks down the cell structure. The prawns, accordingly, become dry in taste and flabby in texture.

A reasonable amount of glaze is 2 oz per 16 oz. Thus a 1lb pack should weigh 14 oz when defrosted correctly.

Gourds Stuffed with Prawns
In India this dish is made with bitter gourds. When these cannot be found elsewhere, small cucumbers may be used instead.

    12 gourds
    1 onion, peeled and chopped
    3 cloves garlic, peeled
    3 dried red chillies
    ½ tsp CORIANDER
    ½ tsp turmeric
    8 oz peeled prawns
    1 tomato, peeled and chopped
    Lemon juice

Bisect the gourds or cucumbers lengthways and scoop out the seeds. Salt them well, or steep them in salty water, to remove the bitterness.

Prepare a masala from the onion, garlic, chillies, coriander and turmeric, either in a mortar or in a blender. Fry the masala in oil or GHEE for about 10 minutes, then add the prawns and tomato, and cook for 3 minutes. Moisten with lemon juice and leave this stuffing to cool.

Finally, stuff 12 gourd halves with the shrimp mixture, put the other halves on top of them, and tie each pair with string. Fry them on both sides in very hot oil or ghee for about 3 minutes on each side or until hot right through.

Grilled Prawns

    4–5 large prawns per person, peeled but uncooked if possible
    Onion(s), peeled and cut into 1 inch squares
    Green pimento, seeded and cut into 1 inch squares
    Red pimento, seeded and cut into 1 inch squares
    Grilling butter made as follows:

Clarify 1 lb butter, reserving all the milk solids (see GHEE). Put all the milk solids and a quarter of the melted butter itself with 2 tsps cumin seed, 2 tsps oregano and one tab paprika into a mixer. Blend until smooth.

Skewer the prawns, altenating them with pieces of onion and pimento. Brush them liberally with the grilling butter.

Under or over high heat, grill them for 5–7 minutes on each side, basting as often as possible.

Greg Morton, whose recipe this is, serves the brochettes on pasta tossed with olive oil, garlic and parsley, or on a pilaff which includes some wild rice.

Grilled Prawns (Another Way)

    1 lb large raw prawns, shelled and deveind
    ¼ pint SOY sauce
    3 tabs medium to sweet sherry

Boil soy sauce with sweet sherry.

Skewer the prawns and brush them with the soy mixture. Grill them fast, about 3 minutes on each side, basting frequently. As with other brochette-type procedures, this Japanese version allows for pieces of pimento, onion, mushroom (or bamboo shoot) being interspersed with the prawns.

Grated ginger, about 1 tab, may be added to the soy and sherry mixture.

Grilled Prawns (a Third Way)

In this recipe, the prawns are not shelled. It comes from the west coast of India, near Cochin, where it is no problem to obtain raw, Mogul-sized prawns.

For 2 lb large prawns, make a paste out of 4 oz melted butter (preferably GHEE) and the following aromatics: 3 bay leaves, 12 cloves peeled garlic, 1 tab fennel seed or aniseed, 1 tsp cayenne, 2 tsps salt, 2 tsps onion seed, 1 tab turmeric, 2 tabs ground CORIANDER, 10 cardamoms and the juice of 4 limes (3 lemons will do). Use the blender for this, and do not worry too much if you cannot remember just where you left your onion or fennel seed.

Wash the prawns. Loosen the shell on the underside and score the flesh with a sharp knife. Rub some of the paste on to and into the prawns, that is between shell and flesh. Leave for 3–4 hours.

Rub some more paste on to the prawns, then grill them for about 5 minutes on each side.

Grune Krabbensuppe
A German soup which combines peas and prawns.

Fat smoked bacon, about 3 oz
2 carrots, sliced
2 onions, peeled and sliced
2 pints chicken stock, FISH STOCK, PRAWN STOCK or water
1 lb shelled peas (frozen will do)
1 tsp summer savory
1 tsp tarragon
¼ pint white wine
8 oz peeled, cooked prawns

Boil the bacon, carrots and onion in the stock for 15 minutes, then discard the bacon. Add the peas and herbs. Cook until all vegetables reach a purée-able consistency, then rub the soup through a sieve. It should be fairly thick and very green. Return it to the heat, add the wine, and when almost simmering, the prawns. Simmer for 1 minute and then serve.

Gulf Shrimp
2 large onions, peeled and chopped finely
6 cloves garlic, peeled and chopped finely
5 stalks celery, chopped finely
4 tabs fruity olive oil
½ tsp saffron
¼ pint dry vermouth
1 14 oz can plum TOMATOES
Salt, black pepper, paprika, cayenne
1 lb shrimp, preferably large ones, uncooked

Fry onion, garlic and celery in olive oil. When the onions are transparent, add the crumbled saffron, and sauté for 2 minutes before deglazing with the vermouth. Then add the tomatoes, cover the pan and simmer for 25 minutes. Add salt and peppers to taste.

This is a classic Americo-Caribbean base for fish, crustaceans and bivalves. The prawns should be poached in it for as long as they need – 2–10 minutes according to their size and state. Other fish or shellfish may be added at the same time, as may spicy sausages or pre-baked pieces of chicken. With prawns, mussels, clams, chicken and sausage all together, 'Heaven', claims Greg Morton, whose recipe this is, 'will appear before your eyes.'

Gumbo

2–3 lb unshelled prawns
1 pint olive or vegetable oil
3 onions, peeled and chopped
3 pimentos, peeled and chopped
3 stalks celery, chopped
3–4 lb okra (ladies' fingers), chopped
1 tab vinegar
8 TOMATOES, peeled
1 tsp cayenne
1 tsp black pepper
1 tsp white pepper
Salt
2 pints FISH STOCK
2 tabs dark ROUX
2 tabs (or more) parsley
6 spring onions

Make PRAWN STOCK with shells and heads of the prawns, by cooking them in fish stock or water for 45 minutes.

Heat the oil. Add the onions, pimentos and celery. After 10 minutes' slow cooking, add the okra, vinegar, peeled tomatoes, the three different types of pepper, some salt and 1½ pints stock. Stir well and simmer the mixture, covered, for 30 minutes. When the okra is tender, stir in the dark roux and a further ½ pint stock. Cook slowly for another 30–45 minutes.

The mixture is now ready for the prawns themselves, but will improve if kept in refrigerator or larder until the following day and then re-heated. Cook the prawns for 5–7 minutes if they are raw, or 2 minutes if already cooked; add parsley and chopped spring onions, and serve with rice.

— Hotel Miami
San Carlos de la Rapita

Habitats

Very small shrimps sometimes use sponges as apartment houses. Others make nests out of seaweed, or indulge in commensal squats by leave of obliging molluscs. The largest species usually put up with sand or mud, whether in shallow or deep waters.

Crustaceans in general are remarkably adaptable. They are found in the coldest waters of the Arctic and Antarctic and at depths of 3½ miles, where the pressure is about four tons per square inch, but also in thermal waters of 100-130°F. They can live in fresh or brackish water, in the sea and in lakes of intense salinity.

Haliporoides triarthrus

The knife shrimp, an esteemed six-inch species found off the east coast of southern Africa, especially Mozambique, where many of them used to find their way into prawns PIRI PIRI, one of the world's great seafood dishes. Since independence from Portugal, if reports be true, Mozambique's huge catch has largely been appropriated by the USSR. The high cost of freedom, but perhaps prawn perestroika is on its way.

A large prawn of the same genus (*Haliporoides diomedeae*) is found off Chile. The sensible fellow protects himself from commercial exploitation by living about 4,500 feet below sea level.

Hermaphrodism

Pandalus borealis, the North Atlantic prawn, is hermaphrodite, in that it starts life as a male but changes to female roughly half-way through its life span.

These prawns spawn in the autumn and protect their eggs from the North Atlantic winter by keeping them beneath their bodies until they hatch in the spring. With warm-water species, hatching takes place within a few weeks of spawning.

Himalayan Prawns

1 lb unpeeled cooked prawns
1 oz butter
1 oz flour
¼ pint cream
½ pint strong sweet beer
Lemon juice or vinegar
Salt and pepper

Make a stock with the heads and shells of the prawns (or add them to an existing FISH STOCK). Make a ROUX with the butter and flour. Add fish stock slowly to the roux, stirring out the lumps. Add cream and simmer for 2–3 minutes before adding the beer and the lemon juice or vinegar (1 scant tab). Also add salt and pepper. Simmer for 10 minutes, before pouring the sauce over a dish of prawns. Sprinkle with breadcrumbs, and finish under the grill.

Hot Malayee Fried Prawns

2 large onions, peeled and chopped
6 cloves garlic, peeled and chopped
3 curry leaves
1 oz fresh ginger, finely chopped
Vegetable oil
1 tsp crushed black peppercorns
1 tsp mustard seed
1 tsp fenugreek
1 tab CORIANDER powder
1 tsp turmeric
10 dried red chillies
TAMARIND water or juice of 2 lemons
4 fresh green chillies
2 lb headless, unpeeled, uncooked prawns
1 small tsp salt
1 small tsp sugar

Fry onions, garlic, curry leaves and ginger in oil. Separately fry black pepper, mustard seed, fenugreek, coriander and turmeric. Grind the dried chillies into a paste with tamarind water; chop the fresh chillies.

Add the red chilli paste and the green chopped chillies to the onion mixture. Fry for 3 minutes. Add the prawns, the separate spice mixture, curry leaves, salt and sugar. Barely cover with a mixture of water and tamarind water and cook until most of the liquid is absorbed and the prawns are tender. If you have to use pre-cooked prawns, add the acidulated water first and simmer the sauce for 10–15 minutes before adding the prawns.

Hot Prawn Salad

1 large cucumber
4 oz mushrooms

Butter
1 tsp flour or cornflour
¼ pint chicken stock
¼ pint cream
Salt and pepper
SOY sauce
4 oz cooked, shelled prawns
Fresh herbs to garnish

Cut the cucumber, washed but not peeled, into large dice, and blanch in boiling water.

Slice the mushrooms and cook them in butter for 3 minutes, using a fairly deep-sided pan. Add the cucumber and sprinkle in flour or cornflour. Mix well. After 2 minutes, gradually add the chicken stock and bring it to a simmer. Then add the cream. Season with salt, pepper and soy. 2–3 minutes before serving the salad, add the prawns and let them heat through in the simmering mixture.

Transfer to a pretty vegetable dish, sprinkle the top with chopped mint or chives (or both), and serve as a first course at dinner, or as a simple lunch to be followed by cheese.

Hotel Miami, San Carlos de la Rapita

The LANGOSTINOS caught at the mouth of the Ebro in Spain are said to be the best in the world, and form the basis of a prawn feast, or LANGOSTINARA, at the Hotel Miami. This is a five-course meal, each course of which is langostinos cooked in a different way.

-Indian Woman preparing Seafood-

Iceland

Fishing is the main industry of this reluctantly beautiful island, and prawns the jewels which should adorn its kroner (instead of capelin which are only edible by the Japanese). True, its rivers still seethe with salmon (for which anglers pay as much as £1,000 per day), its seas also provide cod, haddock and pollock, halibut and red fish – other ranks rather than officer material even if prices have been upped, and whale steaks, as prepared in Reykiavik, can be a revelation, but it is the little North Atlantic prawn which puts Iceland on the gastronomic map. If only she/he (see HERMAPHRODISM) were a little bigger...

Pandalus borealis is probably at its best eaten raw, nay LIVE, when just taken from the seabed. To do this you have to be in the right place at the right time, and while I expect a large number of readers will immediately book flights on Icelandair, the notes which follow will have to suffice for the majority, since seats are in short supply.

The Icelandic prawn-fishing industry can be divided into three sections: fjordur (in-shore) trawling; deep-sea fishing without freezer plant; deep-sea fishing with freezing apparatus on board.

Fjordur fishing involves smallish trawlers going out by day and usually returning to port at night. It is impracticable to fish in the dark since prawns swim up towards the surface at night and are almost impossible to locate in any quantity.

Deep-sea fishing means larger boats and either expeditions of 4–5 days, with 8–10 tons of ice on board, to keep the catch cool, or expeditions of 3–4 weeks, with equipment to freeze the catches.

From fjordur or deep sea, the North Atlantic prawn is perhaps the most visually attractive of all prawn species when just caught. Instead of the rather drab colourless greys and browns of others in the raw state, it is a bright red-pink right from the start, and at the same time translucent. It gleams and tempts.

In normal Icelandic temperatures (below 50°F) prawns remain in good condition, if lightly iced for five days, but, alas, they gradually lose most of their translucent magic. They remain pink, but the flesh within the shell goes more or less opaque. This is unfortunate for Iceland's economy, as they would surely sell at a premium if they kept their original allure. And goodness knows, Iceland has few other natural resources – geysers, waterfalls, lava. Poor Iceland is stern and wild, yet with a per capita gross domestic product significantly higher than the United Kingdom, Federal Germany or the United States, somehow it manages to survive.

Indian Dishes

See DALNA, FRIED PRAWNS, GOURDS STUFFED WITH PRAWNS, GRILLED PRAWNS, HIMALAYAN PRAWNS, JHINGA BHAJI, JHINGA MOLEE, JHINGA TURCARI, PRAWN CURRY, PRAWN PATIA, PRAWN PATURI, PRAWN VINDALOO, PRAWNS IN DARK SAUCE and TANDOORI PRAWNS.

Indonesian Prawn Sambal

The Indonesian archipelago is an important source of prawns, ranging from up-market giants to tiny shrimp which are used for TRASI (shrimp paste) or drying. As in Malaysia, prawn dishes are fiery: chillies are omnipresent; garlic and ginger extremely common; TAMARIND water is often the souring agent; COCONUT MILK a sweetener; and trasi a taste enhancer.

> 3 cloves garlic, peeled and chopped
> 1 onion, peeled and chopped
> 6 CURRY leaves
> 2 fresh chillies (or more)
> Vegetable oil
> 1 tsp SAMBAL OELEK
> 1 tsp oriental shrimp paste (trasi for preference)
> 1 lb peeled prawns
> 1 cup COCONUT MILK
> 1 tsp sugar

Fry garlic, onion, curry leaves and chillies in oil till the onion is soft. Add sambal oelek and trasi; fry on for a few seconds. Add prawns and stir-fry for seconds or minutes according to whether or not they are already cooked. Add coconut milk and sugar. Cook rapidly until the sauce begins to thicken.

This sambal is eaten with rice, with or without other dishes.

Intestine
See DEVEINING.

Iodine

Do not eat any prawns or shrimps which smell of iodine or ammonia because it is a sure sign that they are unfit for human consumption.

J

(Creole Jambalaya)

Jambalaya

A Creole favourite which can be made either by cooking rice and then adding to it a mixture of onions, pimentos, shrimp, ham and sausage (which is how Raymond Thomas Sr, head chef of the French Market Seafood House, New Orleans, does it) or, more persuasively, by cooking the rice with a good many of the ingredients, though not with the shrimp perhaps. Jambalaya can be made with long-grained rice, but is probably better with risotto rice.

Olive oil
8 oz smoked ham cut in small chunks
8 oz chorizo or smoked sausage, in chunks
1 large onion, peeled and sliced
1 large green pimento, chopped
1 stalk celery
3 cups rice
6 cups chicken stock, FISH STOCK or water
6 TOMATOES, peeled (or 14 oz can tomatoes)
1 bay leaf
1 tsp oregano
1 tsp thyme
2 cloves garlic, peeled and chopped
Small glass white wine
12 oz shelled prawns

Heat plenty of olive oil in a large pan and fry the ham and sausage chunks till golden. Remove them and fry the onion, pimento and celery for 5 minutes. Add the rice and fry gently, stirring, for 2–3 minutes. Heat the chicken stock and add it to the rice; also the ham and sausage, the tomatoes, the herbs and the garlic. Cover the pan (it could easily be a cast iron casserole) and cook very slowly for about 25 minutes. All the stock should be absorbed, all the grains of rice separate. Shortly before serving add the glass of white wine and the prawns. Chopped parsley and chopped black olives are useful additions too.

If, by any happy chance, you are using uncooked jumbo prawns for this – jumbolaya – as you would in New Orleans, cook them with the ham at the beginning of the process. Even jumbos, however, should be kept from the rice until it is nearly cooked.

It is perfectly legitimate to increase the quantity of tomato, pimento, ham, shrimp, according to taste or availability. The important thing is to have plenty of meat and vegetables in relation to the rice.

Jhinga Bhaji

8 oz raw shelled prawns
1 onion, peeled and minced
1 clove garlic, peeled and crushed
Fresh ginger
Black pepper
Cumin seed
Garam masala
1 tab CORIANDER leaf
Salt
Flour

Chop the prawns very finely indeed and mix them with the onion and garlic. Flavour this mixture with the spices and coriander – not too strongly, but the actual amount is up to you. Moisten with water and add a little salt. Now add enough flour to give you a rollable consistency. Ideally, use a mixture of chick-pea flour and wheat flour, but if you have no chick-pea flour, just use – flour. Roll the mixture into small balls, then roll the balls in more flour.

Deep-fry the balls, a few at a time, in boiling oil.

Jhinga Molee

This is a mild, white curry suitable for all age groups.

2 onions, chopped finely
2 cloves garlic
1 tsp grated fresh ginger
Oil or GHEE
½ fresh chilli, de-seeded and chopped
1 tsp turmeric
8 CURRY LEAVES
2 cups COCONUT MILK
Salt
1 lb shelled prawns

Fry the onions, garlic and ginger in oil or ghee for 5 minutes, without letting them brown. Add the chilli, turmeric and curry leaves – fry for 1 minute. Add coconut milk and salt – simmer for 10 minutes. Add prawns and cook for 7–10 minutes. If the prawns are already cooked, simmer them for 3 minutes, but lengthen the previous process to 15 minutes.

Jhinga Turcari

1 onion, finely sliced
Oil or GHEE
½ tsp turmeric
½ tsp paprika
½ tsp cayenne
½ tsp black pepper, crushed or milled
1½ tabs ground CORIANDER
½ tsp salt
¼ pint yogurt
1 lb shelled prawns

Fry the onion till golden in oil or clarified butter. Add the turmeric, paprika and cayenne. Fry gently for 5 minutes. Add black pepper, coriander, salt, stirring the new ingredients into the old ones, and cook for a further 2 minutes. Add the yogurt.

The prawns: if using uncooked prawns introduce them to the spices while cooking the turmeric group, just before adding the coriander; if using cooked prawns wait until you have simmered the spices and the yogurt for about 5 minutes. Allow them 2–3 minutes to heat through in the aromatic, not too plentiful sauce.

K

Prawn Kebabs

Kebab

See BLACKENED CAJUN SHRIMP, GRILLED PRAWNS and GULF SHRIMP.

3–4 large uncooked prawns in shell per person.

Make a marinade of oil and lemon juice aromatised with crushed bay leaf, crushed garlic, paprika, cayenne, salt and crushed cardamom.

Loosen the shells on the underside of the prawns and score the flesh with a sharp knife. Work some of the paste between flesh and shell. Marinate the prawns for several hours in the mixture, but keep about half the marinade separate in a covered bowl.

Skewer the prawns.

The prawns may be barbecued and/or grilled. They may also be grilled without skewers. Before cooking them, rub some more marinade on to and into the prawns. Grill them for about 4 minutes on each side.

Kedgeree

I am either the world's leading expert on kedgeree or its biggest bigot. We not only eat it on Good Friday and Christmas Eve, but at Epiphany, Septuagesima, Ascension, Whitsun, Pentecost – and saints' days too numerous to mention.

Kensington's answer to pilaff, paella and risotto, kedgeree has two legitimate forms and a limited number of permitted additives. Prawns are not essential but rank high among the additives. One version is made with smoked haddock, the other with salmon or sea trout. We usually plump for haddock because it's cheaper and just as nice.

1½ lb Finnan haddock on the bone
2 cups long-grained rice
4 eggs
4 oz butter
Black pepper

Stage 1. Poach the haddock in plenty of water for about 12 minutes. When it comes easily away from the bone, lift it out of the water.

Stage 2. Cook the rice in the haddock water. In a separate pan, hard-boil the eggs. Flake the haddock, removing all skin and bones.

Stage 3. Peel and chop the eggs. Drain the rice. Mix rice, fish and eggs together in a large dish, adding plenty of black pepper and butter (preferably melted).

Stage 4. Cover the kedgeree with butter papers from the refrigerator and put it in a fairly hot oven to make up the heat loss at Stage 3.

Permitted additives: whole or shelled prawns or shrimps, SMOKED PRAWNS, cream (at Stage 3), streaky bacon fried crisp, grated cheese (parmesan or mature Cheddar), mussels, turmeric (to colour the rice yellow).

There are serious kedgeree addicts who also add fried onions or garlic. This practice is permitted, but not recommended. Everything else is prohibited.

For salmon kedgeree it is not necessary to cook the rice in salmon water. The salmon may either be poached or cooked in the oven wrapped in aluminium foil – unless, by happy chance, you have sufficient left over from some previous occasion. Otherwise the procedure is the same as for haddock.

Kedgeree is also an appropriate dish for 6 August, the feast of the metamorphosis or transfiguration, a scene originally witnessed by three fishermen – Sts Peter, James and John.

King Prawn

Usually restaurateur hyperbole for the smallest prawn that can be passed off as large. The term should not be used for prawns with counts of more than 25 to the 1lb, unshelled.

Krabbenbrot

Rye bread
Shrimps
Eggs
Butter
Salt and black pepper

Thinly butter one slice of dark rye bread per person. Spread it generously with shrimps. Fry an egg in butter and place it on top of the shrimps. Season with salt and black pepper.

Krabbensuppe

See GRUNE KRABBENSUPPE.

Krill

There are over eighty different species of krill in the Antarctic region, and their numbers are so vast they are said to be virtually inexhaustible. On the other hand, there are reports of dire krill plagues and, of course, threats from pollution. The krill population expanded rapidly at the beginning of this century, as the whale population decreased. If efforts to save the whale succeed, tons and tons of krill will not be saved.

Most krill are very small, but some grow to about 4 inches long, the largest being *Euphasia superba*. With their translucent, six-segmented bodies, krill look – and taste – like small shrimps. In fact, they are shrimp-like crustacea which belong technically to the plankton, though they are able to swim, not drift, and forage for their food.

Krill have sometimes been cast as the last, best hope of an overpopulated, protein-hungry world, but there are formidable obstacles to their exploitation by species other than whales. Fishing conditions in the Antarctic are unpleasant and dangerous, and individual krill, when caught, yield little meat. Their shells are very hard and they are difficult to process on land, let alone at sea in an Antarctic storm. This means that, despite their possibly endless abundance, they cannot be brought cheaply to market. They are most readily processed into a shrimp paste, and some effort is being put into marketing this. The possible use of krill as a foodstuff for salmon farms in the southern hemisphere is also being pursued.

Research and experimentation will doubtless continue. Sooner or later population pressures may force a solution, but humanity probably has a few more years before survival becomes a choice between krill and chastity.

Krupuk

Giant Indonesian crisps made from a batter based on prawns or dried shrimps. They can be bought ready-made from Asiatic stores, but need to be deep-fried for a minute or so before being used. In the frying, they swell up to more than twice their original size. If you cannot find large krupuks, settle for Chinese prawn crackers or follow Alan Davidson's handy recipe for kerupak udang (from *South-East Asian Seafood*):

    1 lb prawns
    1 egg
    2 tabs sugar
    2 lb tapioca flour
    Salt

Grind or mince the prawn meat. Beat the egg, mix it with sugar and add to the ground prawn. Add the tapioca flour and stir the mixture

95

well, adding salted water as you do so. You will need 1½–2 glasses of water to achieve the necessary dough-like consistency.

Shape the dough into a long roll. Put a clean piece of cloth such as a table napkin under it and steam it until the roll is stiff. Then take it out and keep it overnight. Cut it into thin slices the following day. Dry the slices in the sun. They will then be ready for use.

To serve the crackers, heat a generous quantity of oil in a wok, then lower the crackers in one at a time, moving each around with a spatula in such a way as to help it expand to 3 or 4 times its original size while still remaining flat.

L

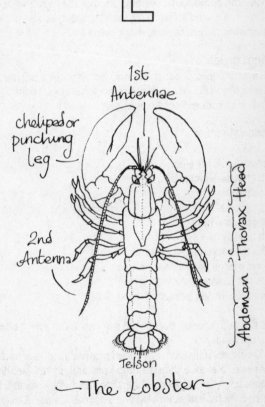

1st Antennae

cheliped or punching leg

2nd Antenna

Abdomen Thorax Head

Telson

—The Lobster—

Langostino, Langostinara

The Spanish word for some of the larger prawns, notably *Penaeus kerathurus*, which is thought by some to be the best eating of all. Thus langostinos are not the same as langoustes or langoustines (for which the Spanish words are langosta and cigala respectively).

The langostinara is a five-course feast in which each dish is based on langostinos. The prawns are served poached, in a sopa, (GAMBAS) A LA PLANCHA, AL RON and MARINARA. Versions of these dishes are given under the appropriate heading, though they are not necessarily the same as those used at the HOTEL MIAMI, SAN CARLOS DE LA RAPITA, where langostinaras are the house speciality.

Langostinos al Ron

Dry the raw, unpeeled langostinos on a hotplate for a minute, then fry them in fine olive oil. When they are cooked, after about 7 minutes, flame them with rum and season with salt.

Langostinos Marinara

3 cloves garlic, peeled
2 tabs toasted almonds
3 tabs parsley
1 tsp paprika
2 tabs tomato purée
1 tab brandy
2 tabs breadcrumbs or croutons
3–4 very large prawns per person
Glass white wine
About 5 clams per person

Blend all the ingredients, except the prawns and clams, adding a little olive oil if necessary.

Fry the large, unpeeled, uncooked prawns for 30 seconds on each side in olive oil. Remove them from the pan and fry the blended sauce. After 5 minutes, add a glass of white wine and a glass of salt water. Stir well and reduce by half before adding 20 small clams. As soon as the clams open, return the langostinos to the pan, and cook for a further 3–4 minutes.

Mussels may be used instead of clams.

Langostinos a la Vinagreta

A simple and delicious Spanish salad which can perfectly well be made with cooked, peeled North Atlantic prawns instead of that marine hidalgo, *Penaeus kerathurus*. It can be served by itself on a bed of lettuce, or included as one element in a more elaborate cold collation.

Make a vinaigrette with 5 tabs good olive oil to 1 tab of wine vinegar. Add 1 tab finely chopped shallot, a finely chopped hard-boiled egg, salt, saffron, cayenne and a small glass Spanish brandy. Mix this well. Fold in the cooked prawns and leave them to marinate for at least 1 hour. A scattering of chopped parsley or chives will do no harm to the final presentation.

Langostinos a la Catalana
Though originally made with langoustes or lobster, this dish is just as good with any large prawn.

        1 onion, peeled and chopped
        Olive oil
        Bay leaf, thyme
        1 lb large prawns, shell on, headless, uncooked if possible
        2 cloves garlic, peeled
        2½ oz cooking chocolate, not sweetened
        10 toasted hazelnuts
        Parsley, chopped
        Saffron
        2 tabs breadcrumbs
        1 tab Spanish brandy
        White wine
        Triangles of fried white bread

Fry the onion in oil with bay leaf and thyme. Do not brown. Add the prawns, if uncooked, and fry gently till they have turned colour on both sides. Remove them with the onion from the heat to an ovenproof earthenware dish.

In a mortar or mixer, blend the garlic, chocolate, hazelnuts, parsley, pinch of saffron and breadcrumbs. Add brandy and dilute with white wine so that you have a medium thick sauce. Pour the sauce over the prawns. Bake in a medium oven for 15 minutes. Serve the prawns, in their earthenware dish, decorated with triangles of fried bread.

Langoustine
See DUBLIN BAY PRAWNS, NEPHROPS NORVEGICUS.

Leek and Prawn Salad

6–8 young leeks
8 oz cooked, shelled prawns
Mayonnaise thinned with single cream
Salt and white pepper
2–3 hard-boiled eggs
Paprika

Cut the well-washed leeks into juliennes about twice as long as match-sticks, including as much of the green part as possible. Blanch them in boiling water. After 1 minute, drain them and plunge them in very cold water. Then drain them again, and get them as dry as possible with absorbent paper or a teacloth. Arrange them in reasonably straight lines over the bottom of an oblong serving dish.

Fold prawns into the mayonnaise and cream mixture. Season with salt and freshly ground white pepper. Spoon the mixture on to the leeks.

Remove the egg yolks from the whites. Dice the whites as finely as possible. Sieve the yolks. Arrange the yolk along the middle of the prawn mayonnaise and scatter the whites on either side. Dust the whites with paprika.

Live Prawns

Not for the squeamish, perhaps, but NORTH ATLANTIC PRAWNS just taken from the sea are as good as oysters, and a lot sweeter. Pull off the head, hold body by tail fan – and bite; alternatively remove both head and shell with fingers before biting. Throw debris over the side.

A virologist informs me that no trace of salmonella has ever been found in North Atlantic prawns. Warm-water prawns, however, are not necessarily so bacteria-free, and may also harbour the lung fluke parasite (though that is more commonly found in crabs), so on your next trip to Bali make sure that all your crustaceans are thoroughly cooked.

Lomo de Camarones

8 oz raw prawns, shelled
2–3 cloves garlic, peeled
1 egg
Breadcrumbs
3 lb boned pork joint, preferably loin

Salt and pepper
Butter
Dry white wine
Arrowroot

Finely chop the prawns and mix them with crushed garlic. Beat the egg and add it to the prawns. Stiffen this stuffing with a scattering of breadcrumbs.

Make large, deep holes all over the pork joint and fill them with the prawn mixture. Season the joint generously. Brown it on all sides in butter, using a deep-sided casserole. When browned, add sufficient white wine to come just over half-way up the joint. Bring the wine up to simmering point, then transfer casserole to a medium-to-low oven, having first covered the meat with foil and put the lid on. Braise slowly for 2 hours.

Remove the meat when cooked to a warm platter. Spoon most of the fat from the cooking liquor. Refresh the liquor with a glass of white wine and boil briskly for 5 minutes. Then thicken the sauce slightly by adding 1 heaped tsp arrowroot previously mixed with a little cold water into a thin paste.

Carve the meat into thick slices. Moisten them with some of the sauce. Serve the rest separately.

Luminosity

A number of crustacea are luminous. Their light-emitting organs, photophores, contain luciferin, a protein-like substance which is oxidised by the enzyme luciferase to produce the light. Remarkably, the process is independent of the body, for luminous substances may be removed, dried, extracted with ether or treated in other ways – and retain their power of producing light for months, even years. During the Second World War, Japanese officers were able to read messages in the dark by light given off from dry pieces of the ostracod *Cypridina hilgendorfi*. (Ostracods are a primitive sub-class of crustacea whose tiny bodies and limbs are enclosed in bivalve shells; they are usually parthenogenetic.)

Of the higher crustacea, at least two prawn species, *Heterocarpus alphonsi* and *Aristeus coruscans* have been found to pour out 'copious clouds of a ghostly blue light of sufficient intensity to illuminate a bucket of sea water so that all its contents were visible in the clearest detail'.

Why do they want to do it? Various theories have been advanced: to attract prey; to attract other individuals of the same species in order to swarm; to attract the opposite sex; to frighten or confuse the enemy; to see objects in the absence of light.

Sometimes crustacea are infected by luminous bacteria. One such species is the fresh-water shrimp *Xiphocaridina compressa*. When infected it glows with such intense inward light that 20 or 30 shrimps in a test-tube make an otherwise dark room bright enough to read in – but once infected by the bacteria they only have a few hours to live. They die in a blaze of glory. From Waldo Schmitt, *Crustaceans*.

See also ZOOLOGISTS AT NIGHT.

M

The Sea Enchantress

Machrobrachium rosenbergii
See FRESHWATER PRAWNS.

Maine Clambake
As a change from prawn cookery, here is a very good way of dealing with lobsters, clams – and Sunday newspapers.

Greg Morton writes:

There are many variations of the clambake, countless procedures, techniques and ingredients. There is one constant, however. The shellfish is cooked (steamed) in seaweed (rockweed) burned by a wood fire, and this way takes on a flavor that is revered by many, especially in the north-east United States. I will describe the bake my family and I make on the rocks at Linekin Bay, Bayville, Maine.

20–30 logs of dry hard wood

Kindling wood

2 Sunday newspapers, no color or magazine sections

Iron or heavy gauge steel plate at least 2 foot by 3 foot with a 2 inch lip around the edge (which helps maintain rigidity and retains water for conversion into steam). If you have a plate specially fabricated, make it 2 foot by 4 foot, with 12 inch legs

2 refuse cans full of fresh seaweed. Use hands or a steel rake to pull weed off the rocks at low tide

1 live lobster per person (or 2 small ones)

1–1½ lb steamer clams per person

Sweetcorn on the cob, 1 or 1½ per person, husks on, silk removed. If corn is not available, wrap some par-boiled red new potatoes in individual pouches with butter, dill and salt

Drawn or clarified butter

Clam juice for dipping (reserve 2 lb clams to make broth)

Gloves and tongs to handle hot seaweed and serve the bake

Large disposable platters for food

Spare refuse can

Tabasco, Worcestershire sauce, horseradish, lemons – to create on-site custom dipping sauces

Cheesecloth for wrapping the clams

Blueberry cake

Theory: to prepare a very hot fire that will heat the cooking plate that will burn the weed that will create the steam that will cook the food. A cross-section from top to bottom:

Wet newspaper (as a lid)
Seaweed
Clams
Seaweed
Corn or potatoes or both
Seaweed
Lobsters
Seaweed
Hot steel plate
Fire

The fire should be set and lit 2 hours before eating time, and be large enough to heat the entire cooking area. It cannot be too hot. Before you start, the plate must be so hot that spittle jumps on it. After 45 minutes and a good restoking of wood, the fire should be ready for the bake.

Now execute the cross-section. Set a 12 inch layer of wet seaweed on the plate (all layers of the bake must be level). Place the lobsters on top of the weed and cover immediately with another layer of weed, 10–12 inches. Sweetcorn is next, then another layer of weed. Lastly the clams wrapped in individual cheesecloth bags in batches of about 1 lb each. Then the final layer of seaweed. The next step is crucial. Place wet sheets of newspaper over the entire bake. They should overlap each other, seal the bake, and ensure steaming. Throw extra seawater on them from time to time.

N.B. You will have to discourage the lobsters' all too understandable desire to escape from the heat. And you must be very careful to keep the whole bake level.

The bake will take 45–50 minutes, and will produce a small but satisfying roar. When it is ready, disassemble it slowly using gloves and tongs. Place the different foods on platters or plates, and use the weed to keep the food hot. Serve with melted butter, clam juice, tabasco and so on.

A better way of using Sunday newspapers has yet to be devised.

Cold beer is in order, but if you have followed these instructions, and it is your first bake, champagne is a must.

For the blueberry cake:

4 cups flour
½ tsp salt
1 cup sugar
2 tsps baking powder

10 oz blueberries (frozen will do fine)
3 large eggs
1¾ cups milk
½ cup melted butter

Combine flour, salt, sugar and baking powder. Add the blueberries. Mix the eggs, milk and butter. Add the wet mixture to the dry to form a batter. Put batter in a cake pan and bake at 375°F for 15–20 minutes.

Mango Salad
It may have been Christian Germain of the Château de Montreuil who discovered how to make a form of mayonnaise substituting mango flesh for egg yolk.

2 ripe mangoes
½ pint olive oil
Salt and pepper
Lemon juice
2 avocados
Selection of salad leaves, of which one should be reddish.
    Rocket and mustard could be included, or purslane
1 lb cooked, peeled prawns

Peel 1 mango, cut it in half and remove the stone. Whizz the flesh in a blender until smooth. Add olive oil, drop by drop at first as for mayonnaise. Season with salt and pepper, and a touch of lemon juice. Do not worry if the final sauce is somewhat runnier than best home-made mayonnaise.

Peel and de-stone the other mango and the avocados. Cut them into segments about the size and shape of an orange pig.

Mix the washed and dried salad leaves with the mango and avocado, taking care not to be too rough. Dress with approximately half of the mango mayonnaise.

Divide the salad between 4, 5 or 6 plates. Put a portion of prawns in the centre of each salad helping and spoon a little more of the mayonnaise over them.

Marinated Prawns
This is a form of ceviche which calls for Seville (bitter) orange juice rather than lemons or limes.

1 onion, peeled and chopped finely
1–2 chillies, chopped finely
1 large tomato, peeled and chopped finely
½ pint Seville orange juice
1 lb prawns, peeled and cooked

Mix the onion, chilli and tomato in a bowl with the orange juice and the prawns. Season with salt and pepper. Marinate for a minimum of 1 hour.

The prawns can be served, with most of their marinade, on a bed of salad materials, in a half avocado, or with chick peas which, after being boiled till tender, have been fried crisp in olive oil and lightly seasoned with salt and cayenne.

Matelote de Crevettes

Matelotes are the classic fresh-water fish casseroles of France, so fresh-water prawns are appropriate here. However, marine species can be used perfectly well.

1 lb large, unshelled prawns
2 large onions, peeled and sliced, or 12 pickling onions
1 clove garlic, peeled
2 oz butter
1½ oz flour
½ bottle cheap, dry white wine
Bouquet garni
2 mushrooms, chopped
Salt and pepper
1 tab brandy

Broil the prawns (see GAMBAS A LA PLANCHA) – in a slatted, heavy-bottomed pan over very high heat, for 2 minutes on each side. When they are cool enough, remove their shells. If they are large, bisect each prawn.

Melt the onion and garlic in butter for 5 minutes. If using whole, little onions, fry them gently for at least 10 minutes. Add flour to make a light ROUX. Loosen the roux with white wine, slowly at first, stirring out potential lumps, then more quickly. Add the prawn shells and the bouquet garni. Simmer for 12–15 minutes, then fish out the prawn shells and bouquet. Add the mushrooms and the prawns. Season with salt and pepper; flare with the brandy. Simmer for 5 minutes.

Remove the prawns and keep them warm on a serving dish. Reduce the liquor in the pan by boiling briskly for another 5 minutes. Then, when it has thickened a little, pour it over the prawns, and serve with boiled potatoes.

Large croûtons of white bread make a pleasant garnish, as do hard-boiled eggs. The brandy may be omitted.

Mazzancolla
Italian for PENAEUS KERATHURUS, the largest and most prized Mediterranean prawn. 'Every bit as good [as scampi], if not better,' Elizabeth David, *Italian Food*.

Melanosis
This is a disfiguring but harmless and tasteless complaint which can attack prawns within hours of their being caught. Black patches develop around the neck and gradually spread. Eventually they can affect the meat itself. A BORIC ACID dip prevents melanosis, but is no longer permitted in most countries. Citric acid is less effective, but sometimes used. Careful handling and rapid chilling inhibit 'black spot', and today most prawns are frozen before melanosis starts.

Mexican Shrimp
A chilli-free dish from Acapulco.

> 1 lb unpeeled prawns, raw if possible
> Parsley stalks
> 2 oz butter
> 2 cloves garlic, chopped
> 4 tabs parsley
> 3 TOMATOES, peeled and chopped
> 3 tabs tomato paste
> 5 tabs brandy

Remove heads and shells from the prawns and use these to make stock with 15 fl oz water and some parsley stalks. Boil, with lid off for about 20 minutes, reducing the volume to about ½ pint.

Fry garlic and 2 tabs parsley in butter for 3 minutes, without burning or browning. Add the tomatoes and cook for 10 minutes. Stir in and amalgamate the tomato paste before adding the prawn stock and the brandy. Simmer for 5 minutes. Add the prawns and cook them in the sauce for 2–7 minutes according to their size and to whether or not they are raw.

Molho de Pimenta e Limao

A Brazilian relish guaranteed to pep up faded stews and jaded palates.

    4 fresh chillies
    1 clove garlic, peeled
    1 onion, peeled
    1 tsp salt
    Scant ¼ pint lime or lemon juice

Chop the chillies, garlic and onion very small. Pound them in a mortar with the salt. Add the lime juice gradually. Pour the mixture into a blender and whizz for a second or two.

Mousses aux Crevettes

Since one eats prawns as much for their texture as for their taste, it seems a pity to render them into mousses or fish balls. Better surely to make a mousse with some inexpensive white fish and either garnish it with prawns or serve it with a shrimp sauce?

As sauce for a hot fish mousse: melt a 2 oz carton of POTTED SHRIMPS in a little butter stir in a little cream and sharpen with lemon juice. Season with red pepper.

Alternatively, make a sauce mousseline (3 parts hollandaise to 1 part cream), incorporating peeled shrimps.

For a cold mousse, make BÉARNAISE sauce and add peeled shrimps.

Moulting

All crustaceans moult, that is to say they cast off their old shells and grow new ones whenever they need to. They do this particularly when they are growing. Indeed it is moulting which enables them to grow. Once fully grown, they moult infrequently. They eat their cast-off shells as a source of calcium. This moulting process is called ecdysis – sometimes a useful word at dinner parties.

N

Noodles

Nage

Nage and COURT BOUILLON are usually considered interchangeable terms for the vegetable-flavoured broth in which fish and shellfish should be poached, but sometimes the former word is applied to the liquor only when fish has been cooked in it, in short, when it is fish-flavoured. The nage can be served, perhaps after reduction, as a sauce in its own right. Alternatively, it can be used as a constituent of other sauces and fish soups.

Nam Prik

Made with dried prawns and dried shrimp paste, this sauce, in various forms, is ubiquitous in Thailand. The other ingredients are garlic, chillies, lemon juice, sugar and soy.

Nam prik can be used as a sauce or dip for raw or lightly cooked vegetables, hard-boiled eggs, fried fish or chicken. It should be used sparingly until the strong, fishy taste is acquired.

Nantua Sauce

Although Constance Spry roundly translates this as prawn sauce, most authorities insist that 'Nantua' implies the presence of écrevisses. With either crustacean it remains one of the best sauces for cod, haddock, halibut or the grander white fish.

> BÉCHAMEL SAUCE
> PRAWN BUTTER
> Double cream
> Peeled prawns

Use equal quantities of PRAWN STOCK and milk when making the bechamel sauce. Then enrich it with 3 tabs cream and 2 oz prawn butter per ½ pint sauce. Finish with a few peeled, cooked prawns.

Nephrops norvegicus

See SCAMPO.

Newburg

One of the classic ways of preparing lobster or langouste. It adapts without embarrassment to large prawns, and makes a very stylish, rather old-fashioned dish.

For 4 people as a main course:

> 1 lb peeled prawns, very large if possible

1½ oz butter
Scant ¼ pint dry sherry
½ pint double cream
3 egg yolks

Toss the prawns in butter over heat for a couple of minutes. Sprinkle them with the sherry and let the sherry reduce by at least half as it liaises with the butter. Cover the prawns with cream and bring up to simmering point. If using pre-cooked prawns, remove the pan from the heat 1 minute after the cream has started simmering. Uncooked prawns will need another 3–4 minutes' cooking.

Finish the sauce by thickening it with egg yolks over a very low heat. It is probably more convenient to transfer the prawns to their serving dish before incorporating the eggs.

Noodles
Apart from spaghetti alle vongole, one of Italy's great dishes, most pasta and fish combinations seem to be of recent origin and to have designer food status. Those who regard pasta primarily as a cheap, filling vehicle for grated parmesan and red wine must view its up-marketisation, particularly by restaurants, with healthy cynicism. It has to be admitted, however, that pasta can be a good medium for stretching expensive seafood, and it could perfectly well be argued that such stretchings are in keeping with thrifty peasant tradition and therefore do not constitute culinary gentrification. See NOUILLES AUX CREVETTES ET MOULES.

North Atlantic Prawns
Pandalus borealis. This is the principal cold-water species, and the one most easily found in British shops. It is native to British waters and there are important fisheries in the waters of Norway, Iceland, Greenland and Canada. Related species are found in Alaska and northern Asia.

Cold-water prawns take longer to grow than their warm-water cousins, and their slow maturation is reckoned by some experts to endow them with superior flavour and texture. They are certainly better than some of the small tropical prawns which are exported to Europe, but no better than, perhaps not so good as, some of the giants.

North Atlantic prawns can attain a length of over 3½ inches, but they are usually sold at about 1–2½ inches (from 150/250 up to 400/500 to the lb, shelled). It would be interesting to compare a very large one with a tropical prawn of the same size.

Pandalus borealis is hermaphrodite. It starts life male, but changes to female, like Virginia Woolf's Orlando, half-way through its four-year span. The females spawn in the autumn and protect their eggs from the North Atlantic winter by keeping them beneath their bodies until they hatch in the spring.

Warm-water species do not go in for sex changes, and their eggs hatch within weeks of spawning.

Nouilles aux Crevettes et Moules

8 oz unpeeled prawns
½ pint shrimps
1 pint mussels
½ cup dry cider or wine
4 large TOMATOES
Olive oil
Salt and pepper
Cayenne
12 oz noodles
3 tabs cream

Shell the prawns and shrimps. Wash and beard the mussels. Cook the mussels with ½ cup dry cider or wine (or just water) until they open. When cool enough remove the mussels from their shells. Reserve and strain the mussel liquor.

Prepare a NAGE using the mussel liquor, ½ pint water and the prawn and shrimp shells as well as some chopped vegetables. If the prawns are uncooked add them in a strainer to the nage when it has boiled for 20 minutes. Cook them in the nage for 6 minutes and fish them out. Then strain the nage, now well reduced, and discard the vegetables and shells, squeezing the debris to extract as much liquor as possible.

Peel the tomatoes, cut them in half, and quarter each half. Sweat them in olive oil for 10 minutes, seasoning with salt and pepper, also a little cayenne.

Boil the noodles in salted water with a tsp of olive oil. If home-made, they will take 2–3 minutes; if fresh from a pasta shop, about 6 minutes; if packeted, about 12 minutes. Drain them while they are still al dente, and transfer to a very hot dish.

Meanwhile, add cream to the reduced nage and boil briskly. After 2 minutes add the mussels.

Add the tomatoes, prawns and shrimps to the pasta, using two forks to distribute them gently and evenly. Pour the hot cream and mussel sauce over the pasta. Serve as quickly as possible on very hot plates.

Nuptial Swarming

One obscure prawn species, *Callianassa turnerana*, swarms dramatically, and for some of them fatally, every three years, usually in August, at the mouth of the Rio de Camaraõs in Cameroon, West Africa. Sometimes the swarming lasts only a few hours, but it may last as long as a week or ten days. Afterwards, the shrimp disappear as abruptly as they came, as reported by Waldo Schmitt in *Crustaceans*.

While the *mbeatoe* are there, the local people do nothing but fish and feast:

All tribal differences on the coast are forgotten during the grand occasion. Social distinctions, too, are laid aside, and the most lowly may insult even the chief among the notables if he be so minded. As Dr Monod, to whom I am indebted for the genesis of the greater part of this tale, relates, public confessions of personal ills or maladies, and even of one's connubial troubles, seem likewise to be in order. But two stern prohibitions also prevail. Anyone challenged to give his name may be slain if he does not respond to the third demand for such information. This is solely as a precaution against spies and against attacks from the more warlike inland tribes who have in the past taken advantage of 'shrimp week' to perpetrate disastrous raids on the coastal populations. The other taboo concerns the women, for only men may take part in the actual fishing of *mbeatoe*.

The procedure is somewhat as follows: the men wade out waist deep into the water with baskets and canoes. Every dip of the basket in the water means a full take of shrimp. The fishery appears to be prosecuted only in the evening and at night, and, failing moonlight, each of the many boats is provided with its flaming faggot.

In spite of intense excitement prevailing, the entire performance is conducted with religious fervour and with all due regard to precedent. The natives maintain a crude but rhythmic cadence in the dipping of the baskets, keeping time with a barbaric chant ... varied at intervals with direct address to the personification of the shrimp as 'the man of the river'.

Such vast quantities of the crustaceans are consumed that great piles of the discarded carapaces accumulate in all directions, and, rotting under the tropic sun, produce a most awful stench. One wonders whether, after all, it was not the smell rather than the swarming that lingered longest in the memories of the Portuguese navigators who gave the place its name.

See CAMEROON.

Okra — an ingredient of Prawn Creole

Ocopa de Camarones

A hearty Peruvian dish of potatoes and prawns in a cheese and chilli
sauce.

    1 onion, peeled and chopped
    2 cloves garlic, peeled and chopped
    Olive or vegetable oil
    2–6 dried or fresh red chillies
    2 oz walnuts
    12 oz cooked, peeled prawns
    ½ pint warm milk
    4 oz grated cheese
    6 medium potatoes, cooked, peeled and halved
    6 hard-boiled eggs

Gently fry onion and garlic in olive or vegetable oil for 10 minutes. Cut
the chillies in strips and soak them in warm water while the onions are
cooking.

Put the onions, garlic, the oil they were cooked in, the walnuts,
two-thirds of the prawns, chillies, milk and cheese into a blender or
food processor. Blend to a smooth sauce of mayonnaise consistency.
If it seems too thick, add a little more milk and oil in equal quantities.
Transfer sauce to saucepan and heat it through. Then pour it over
the potatoes. Garnish with the remaining prawns and the hard-boiled
eggs cut in half. Also with strips of red pimento, if you like, and black
olives.

Oeufs Durs Norvégienne

    Shortcrust pastry using 6 oz flour
    Oil and vinegar
    Mustard
    Sugar
    Double cream
    8 oz peeled, cooked shrimps or prawns
    5 hard-boiled eggs
    6 anchovy fillets
    1 dill-pickled cucumber (or fresh cucumber)

Line a flan ring with the rolled-out pastry and bake it blind.

In a large bowl make ¼ pint vinaigrette, strongly flavoured with
mustard and generously sweetened with sugar. Stir 2 tabs cream

into the dressing and whisk it energetically. Add the prawns plus the chopped whites of the hard-boiled eggs.

Sieve the yolks through a fine strainer. Cut each anchovy fillet in half lengthways. Slice the cucumber thinly.

When the flan is cold, line it round the perimeter with overlapping slices of cucumber. Then fill it with the prawn and egg-white mixture, using a slatted spoon so that any excess of dressing drains off. Garnish with a lattice of anchovy strips and a ring of egg yolk. Sprinkle with fresh dill, if you like.

This mixture of cucumber, egg and prawn in a mustardy dressing also makes a good open sandwich (or canapé).

Oeufs Farcis

Cut hard-boiled eggs in half. Remove the yolks; mash them with mayonnaise and chopped shrimps or prawns. Then stuff the mayonnaise mixture attractively into the yolk cavities. Serve as canapés or as part of an hors d'oeuvre.

Okra

See DOMINICAN PRAWNS.

Omelettes

Fresh shrimps or small prawns are more appropriate for omelettes than their big brothers, and they should be peeled and pre-cooked. For a 2-egg omelette, heat 1 heaped tab shrimps in butter and moisten them with 1 scant tab cream. Season with the pepper.

Beat and season the eggs. Heat a mixture of butter and oil in an omelette or non-stick pan. Get it very hot. Pour in the egg mixture and stir it with a wooden spoon while shaking the pan vigorously for 30 seconds. With the omelette beginning to set, put the shrimp and cream mixture in the middle and as soon as you are able, fold one side of the omelette over the shrimps, then the other. Slide it out of the pan on to a warm plate. About 90 seconds in all, unless you like your omelettes very well cooked.

Escoffier recommends heating the shrimps in meat jelly rather than butter, and calls the dish omelette Nantua.

For a **Spanish omelette** with prawns a slower process is used. Fry a large, sliced onion in olive oil over fairly gentle heat. Add 1 tsp paprika. After 7 minutes, add 2–3 chopped, skinned TOMATOES and cook them with the onions for another 7 minutes. Then add 2 cubed boiled potatoes. Mix these in well before adding a good sprinkling of shrimps or small prawns.

Beat 4–5 eggs and season them with salt and pepper. Pour the egg on to the other ingredients and use a fork to distribute it evenly. Cook slowly until the egg has set. Large, thick Spanish omelettes may be finished under the grill.

Open Sandwiches

The so-called open sandwich beloved of Norsefolk is a good way of economising on bread. It is not a convenience food to be taken on picnics or to be munched while playing faro, roulette or blackjack, since it requires a knife and fork. The most appropriate time for it, therefore, is at lunch, in particular for the deceptively casual lunch party which is achieved by serious graft in the kitchen.

The important thing is to have the right kind of bread. Neither English nor French will do. The bread must be thinly sliced, but firm, close-grained, slightly moist. For open sandwiches featuring prawns, however, it is best to avoid very dark, pumpernickel-type breads and have the lightest or whitest rye, or partially rye, that you can find. In all cases the bread's texture must be protected from the filling by butter, otherwise it will go soggy. (The Danish word *smorrebrod* in fact means smeared bread, i.e., buttered.)

One of the most attractive open sandwiches is made with peeled shrimps, at least 25 per slice, if possible 40 or 50. Plenty of butter, black pepper or paprika, a squeeze of lemon – no mayonnaise.

Prawn *smorrebrod*, on the other hand, are best with a lubrication of mayonnaise or one of the other PRAWN COCKTAIL sauces. Hard-boiled eggs go well with such mixtures and the sandwich may be topped with a sprinkling of lumpfish roe (or genuine caviar). Mixing the mayonnaise with sour cream is fine, but adding curry paste produces a hybrid which appeals most to those who are ideologically committed to miscegenation (also, it has to be admitted, to Danes).

Oranges
See MARINATED PRAWNS.

Orlando
A soup (or stew) in which seagulls have to render account for all those hitherto free lunches from North Atlantic waters (see FISHING THE FJORDURS). It gives less retaliatory satisfaction made with ordinary eggs, but tastes almost as good.

Shells and heads from at least 1½ lb NORTH ATLANTIC PRAWNS
2 pints milk

6–8 oz cod or haddock, cubed
1 large onion, peeled and quartered
12 oz potato, peeled and diced finely
6 oz swede (or carrot), peeled (scraped) and diced finely
6 gulls' eggs
Liqueur glass Brennewin (aquavit)
2 oz peeled, cooked prawns
Gardener's herbs – optional (see below)

Simmer prawn shells and heads in the milk, together with the cod and the onion, in a covered pan. After 15–20 minutes, strain the milk into another pan; throw away shells and onion.

Cook the potato and swede in the prawny milk until they virtually disintegrate – another 15–20 minutes. Then strain the broth again, pressing most of the vegetables through it (or whizz it in a blender if you wish).

Meanwhile, hard-boil 2 gulls' eggs, and whisk 4 in a bowl. (Bantams' eggs are the same size as gulls'.)

Return broth to pan and add a small glass of Brennewin (or any caraway-flavoured Nordic spirit). Bring to a simmer, then remove from heat. Check seasoning.

Stir a little of the slightly cooled broth into the whisked eggs; then combine the egg mixture with the remainder of the broth. Put saucepan on a very low heat and cook at just under simmering point for 5–7 minutes, stirring occasionally. When the consistency is silky, add a handful of peeled prawns and the hard-boiled eggs finely chopped.

Chopped chives, parsley or dill will give an attractive, if slightly effeminate (well, at any rate non-Viking) speckle to a soup which, with or without herbs, is equally fulfilling in Bloomsbury or the Arctic.

Orlando may be boosted into a main course stew by increasing the potato, swede and prawn content in relation to the milk, and removing some of the vegetables as soon as they are al dente, during their initial simmering. The removed cubes should be returned to the pottage as soon as the egg liaison has been effected.

Paella

Paella

One of the world's better rice dishes, some (not only Valencians) would say the best. Prawns are an essential ingredient, though paella is much more than a prawn dish. The other essential ingredients are mussels, chicken, chorizo, real olive oil, saffron and rice. Rapa (angler fish) is also much favoured in Spain.

> Olive oil
> 3 cloves garlic, coarsely chopped
> 1 large onion, peeled and chopped
> 3 TOMATOES, peeled and chopped
> 1 red pimento, cut into strips
> 1 small chicken cut into small pieces but not de-boned
> Salt, pepper and paprika
> 2 cups round-grained rice
> 8 oz chorizo or Spanish-type cooking sausage (not salami)
> 4 cups chicken stock
> Saffron
> 12 or more mussels
> 12 or more unpeeled prawns

Rabbit, pork, peas and chopped parsley may also be included, as may lobster or langouste on special occasions.

Paella can be made in a very large, deepish frying pan, but if you get hooked on this dish, it will be worth investing in a *paellera*, the Spanish version of a – large, deepish frying pan. Our paellera is 2 inches deep by 16 inches across.

Heat olive oil in the pan and flavour it with the garlic for 3 minutes. Then remove the garlic and add the onion. When the onion is just beginning to turn golden, add the tomatoes, the pimento and the chicken pieces and cook gently for 10 minutes, stirring occasionally. Season with salt, pepper and a generous amount of paprika. Then add the chorizo, cut in small chunks, and the rice. After another good stir, add twice as much chicken stock as rice and a good pinch of saffron. Bring it up to a simmer, and cook for 15 minutes without further stirring. Add the mussels in their shells about half-way through this process and the prawns, if uncooked, at the same time. If the prawns are already cooked, delay their introduction till the end. The paella is ready when all the liquid has been absorbed but the rice is still moist. Shortly before the dish is served, it should, according to some authorities, be sprinkled with sherry.

In sunny Spanish weather, it is delightful to prepare paella outside on a barbecue, still in a paellera if possible, while drinking a cheerful half-pint of wine.

In Spanish Spanish the double-l is pronounced like an English y, so paella ends with a ya sound, not with a la.

Pancakes

2 egg yolks
½ cup double cream
½ tsp salt
¾ cup sifted flour
1 tab melted butter
¾ cup grated parmesan cheese
¾ cup cooked, peeled prawns cut into halves or quarters
2 egg whites

Beat the yolks, stir in the cream and salt. Beat in the flour until smooth, then mix in the melted butter and one-third of the cheese. Chill for an hour, before incorporating the prawns or shrimps.

Beat the egg whites until they are stiff but not dry; fold them into shrimp mixture.

Drop the mixture by the tablespoon on to a hot, well-greased griddle or frying pan. Cook until just brown on both sides. Arrange the pancakes on a buttered fireproof dish and sprinkle them with the remaining cheese. Brown the cheese under the grill.

Pandalus borealis

See NORTH ATLANTIC PRAWNS, ICELAND.

Paprika Prawns

4 shallots, peeled and chopped
Butter
1 tab paprika
1 tab tomato purée
16 large (headless, shell on) prawns
2 tabs brandy
4 tabs dry white wine
4 tabs cream
Salt
Tarragon

Soften the shallots in butter for about 5 minutes over low to moderate heat. Add paprika and mix well. Add tomato purée. After 2 minutes add the prawns. Cook them 2 minutes each side before flaring them with brandy. When the flames die down, add wine, and simmer briskly for 3 minutes, again turning the prawns over at least once. Then remove the prawns to a hot serving dish.

Add the cream to the sauce left in the pan. Thicken by brisk boiling (3–5 minutes) and season with salt. Before pouring this over the prawns fleck it with chopped tarragon.

Penaeidea

The infra-order to which about 80 per cent of the world's commercially significant prawns belong, including PENAEUS KERATHURUS, PENAEUS MONODON, PENAEUS VANNAMEI. They are distinguished from prawns of the CARIDEA, the other main group, by the fact that the second segment of their tails overlaps the third segment but is overlapped by the first.

In so far as there is a league table of prawns, most of the top places belong to *penaeidea* – and most of the bottom places too. At least two caridean species – the North Atlantic prawn and the giant river prawn – are among the league leaders, however.

Penaeus kerathurus

France's CARAMOTE, Italy's MAZZANCOLLA, the true LANGOSTINO – and probably the best prawn in the world. The caramote prawn is found mainly in the Mediterranean and along the west coast of Africa, but sometimes as far north as Cornwall. It grows to more than eight inches in length and is attractively striped. Most of them are hogged by the French, Spanish and Italians for reasons that are all too understandable.

Penaeus monodon

The largest prawn, growing to over twelve inches, and one of the best. It is indigenous to the Indian Ocean and can be found from the east coast of Africa to Australia. Known variously as the giant TIGER PRAWN, black tiger prawn or panda prawn, it is also being farmed with some success. If farming leads to wider availability, so much the better.

Penaeus vannamei

This major commercial species is found on the west coast of America from California to Peru, and known as the whiteleg shrimp. It grows to about nine inches and is farmed with considerable success. Very similar to *Penaeus stylirostris*, which comes from the same area.

Pepper and Pain

Hot and spicy tastes are caused by the chemical stimulation of pain-detecting nerve endings, mostly in the mouth. The active ingredient of black and white pepper is called piperine, and that of red pepper capsaicin. They are two alkaloids very similar in composition and structure, and closely related to zingerone, which is responsible for the taste – or pain – inflicted by GINGER. It is thought that the pleasure some of us derive from hot, spicy food may arise both from the ability of pain-producing compounds to stimulate the release of endorphins in the brain and from the way they stimulate the excretion of saliva. The subject is interestingly discussed in P.W. Atkins, *Molecules*. He describes endorphins as natural analgesics akin to opiates.

Peruvian Pigeon

    6 plump pigeons
    Butter
    1 large onion, peeled and chopped roughly
    1 clove garlic, peeled and chopped
    Flour
    ½ pint white wine
    ¾ pint chicken stock
    Salt and pepper
    Nutmeg
    8 oz peeled prawns
    2 eggs
    Fresh CORIANDER

Brown the pigeons in butter (or a mixture of butter and oil). Transfer them to a large casserole.

In the same butter (and oil) fry the onion and garlic until soft. Add up to 2 tabs flour to make a substantial ROUX, and when it has cooked for 2 minutes, start adding the wine, stirring to make a smooth, lumpless paste. Then add the chicken stock. Season with salt, pepper and nutmeg. Simmer for 5 minutes, then pour the sauce over the pigeons.

Cover the casserole with a well-fitting lid and cook over low heat, or in a low oven, until the birds are very tender, with the flesh almost coming away from the bone – 1–1½ hours.

When they are cooked, lift out the birds and keep them warm on a serving dish.

Add the prawns, chopped in half unless very small, to the sauce in the casserole and simmer them for 5 minutes or heat them through for 2 minutes, according to whether they are raw or cooked.

Remove casserole from the heat and stir the eggs, well beaten, into the sauce. Stir well for 1 minute and taste for seasoning. Add chopped coriander leaf.

Spoon a little of the sauce over pigeons; serve the rest in a sauce boat or small, earthenware pot.

Piri Piri

During the month I worked in South Africa, I developed a very close relationship with prawns – and chicken – piri piri, yet I have never been able fully to probe the secrets of this dish. Of course the principal spice is red chilli, and of course the culinary details vary from kitchen to kitchen and restaurant to restaurant – but is it really as simple as expatriate South Africans insist? Is it just chilli and oil? Is it almost the same if you use tabasco? What exactly is in the so-called piri piri powders and sauces which can be bought (and which, when I have used them, give a result very different from those distant but vividly remembered lunches)? Should parsley or marjoram be included, or a touch of CORIANDER seed? Clearly it is important to keep the aromatisation simple, because one of the great charms of piri piri cooking is that it goes so well with wine – enhances it, in fact – whereas curries, with their multiplicity of spices and complexity of taste (even when they appear quite crude) do nothing for wine, and are usually better with water or beer.

No one should suggest that eating prawns piri piri lends moral support to apartheid. The dish comes from Mozambique, and Mozambique took it from relatively non-racist, albeit colonialist Portugal (where other versions are still to be found).

Here is a piri piri analogue.

Olive oil (not vegetable or nut)
Fresh red chillies (or dried)
1 lb large, uncooked prawns with shell on
Salt
Garlic
Brandy
1 tsp lemon juice
Dry white wine

Heat enough oil to coat the prawns and make a marinade, cooking 2–3 chopped chillies to flavour it. Do not burn the chillies. Allow the oil to cool down to tepid.

Score the underside of each prawn with a sharp knife. Put them all in a bowl and pour the chilli-flavoured oil over them. Add plenty of salt and marinate the prawns for as long as you like, but at least an hour.

After a suitable interval, lightly fry 2 more chillies and just a scrap of garlic in a little more olive oil for 3 minutes. Then add the prawns and their marinade, raising the heat under the frying pan. Cook them for 5–6 minutes, turning them over at the half-way stage.

Flare the prawns with a liqueur glassful of brandy (or cane spirit) before transferring them, with a slatted spoon, to a warm dish.

Add lemon juice to the frying pan and bubble it fast to effect an emulsion. Then add white wine and simmer the resulting sauce for 3 minutes. Add salt. When the sauce has reduced a little, pour it over the prawns. Serve the dish with rice and salad.

Port wine
See CAMAROES COM VINHO DO PORTO.

Potage aux Crevettes

> 1 lb shrimps (or small prawns) in their shells
> Parsley stalks
> Thyme
> 6 shallots, finely chopped
> Butter
> 6 TOMATOES, peeled and quartered
> Salt and pepper
> Anchovy essence
> ½ pint dry white wine or Normandy cider

Shell and de-head the shrimps. Boil heads and shells in water (or FISH STOCK) for 15 minutes, with parsley stalks and thyme.

Melt the shallots in butter. After 7 minutes, add the tomatoes and cook them until they virtually amalgamate with the shallot to form a purée – at least 20 minutes over low heat. Season with salt, pepper and anchovy essence. Stir occasionally.

Incorporate the strained PRAWN STOCK into the tomato mixture and add wine or cider. Simmer for 7–10 minutes; throw in the peeled shrimps and serve.

Potage aux Tomates et aux Queues de Crevettes

This is from Alexandre Dumas as rendered by Alan and Jane Davidson in *Dumas on Food*:

> In one pan, heat salted water for the shrimps, with assorted herbs and 2 slices of lemon. When it is boiling, throw in the shrimps.
>
> In a second pan, put 12 tomatoes from which you have pressed out the excess liquid, 4 big onions cut in rounds, a piece of butter, a clove of garlic and assorted herbs. Cook all this together.
>
> When the shrimps are cooked, drain them in a colander, keeping the cooking water. Peel them and put the peeled tails aside.
>
> Once the tomatoes and onions are cooked, press them through a fine sieve, put them back on the fire with a little jellied meat stock and a pinch of red pepper, and let this thicken into a purée. Then add an equal quantity of bouillon, and half a glass of the water in which the shrimps were cooked; bring to the boil while stirring. When it has boiled up 3 or 4 times, toss in the shrimps, and the soup is ready.

Potted Shrimps

One of the loveliest ways of enjoying CRANGON CRANGON, but one of the fiddlier if you do it yourself. Most people buy them ready potted. Those made by James Baxter & Sons of Morecambe are particularly excellent, and Albert Wharf (London, SW11) selects discriminatingly.

Apart from the peeling (or 'picking' as it is called traditionally), the biggest problem for most home potters will be finding enough pots of the right, 2 oz size. It's possible to put them in bigger pots, of course, but more convenient to have them in separate individual servings.

1 lb shrimps, cooked or uncooked
3–4 oz butter
Black pepper
Cayenne
Salt
Mace or nutmeg

If the shrimps are uncooked, boil them in salted or sea water for 3 minutes. Plunge them at once into ice-cold water. Then drain them and, as with pre-cooked shrimps, remove heads, legs and shells. Reserve the pickings for soup or stock.

Melt half the butter, spicing it with plenty of pepper, a good pinch of cayenne, a little salt and a little powdered mace. Add the shrimps and just heat them through, stirring with wooden spoon.

Pot them into individual 2 oz containers. You will need 3 or 4 for this amount, depending on how conscientious you have been with your picking. Heat the remaining butter and when fully melted but not at all burnt, divide it between the pots. It should cover the shrimps by about one-eighth of an inch when they are flattened and gently pressed with the back of a dessertspoon. Let them set in a cool larder or refrigerator. Remove them to room temperature at least an hour before serving.

With toast and wedges of lemon, potted shrimps make one of the best starters in the repertoire.

Sealed with an extra layer of clarified butter, the shrimps will keep for at least a fortnight.

Prawn Butter

Extremely efficacious and useful as a garnish, a mini sauce or as a finishing touch to soups and stews. Prawn or shrimp butter enhances any simply cooked white fish and makes an excellent canapé in its own right (or with caviar, smoked fish, scrambled eggs, and so on).

For making prawn butter the proportions are 3½–4 oz of butter to 2 tabs shelled and pounded prawn or shrimp meat. Melt the butter gently, stir in the pounded prawn meat, season lightly with pepper (use freshly ground white pepper if possible) and rub it all through a sieve. If pounding is not your forte, use a blender (with discretion). After sieving, refrigerate.

If making 8 oz or more at a time (a good idea since prawn butter is an excellent stand-by, and keeps many days in a fridge and almost indefinitely in a freezer), use a blender for the whole process, and forget about sieving, so long as you make sure no shell is present.

Prawn butters can be characterised and prettified by the addition of seasonal herbs such as parsley, tarragon or dill – or be given extra clout with paprika, cayenne, green or red peppercorns or horseradish. Remember, however, that this also limits their versatility. When you come to use the butter you may not want the forceful presence of horseradish, say, or green peppercorns, or even parsley (if, for example, you are deliberately using basil and do not want a mixed herb effect). A hint of lemon or lime, however, is welcome in most contexts.

Use smallish prawns; shrimps are just as good, perhaps better.

Prawn or Shrimp Butter Made with the Shells

This is more elaborate but a good way of exploiting heads and shells when you have used the meat for another dish.

1½ lb prawn shells and heads
2 tabs olive oil
4 oz carrots, peeled and chopped finely
2 oz celery, chopped finely
2 oz leek, chopped finely
2 oz shallot, peeled and chopped finely
2 cloves garlic, peeled and chopped finely
1 tab tomato purée
1½ lb butter
½ pint water

Using a deep-sided pan or wok, fry the washed and dried shells and heads in olive oil for 3 minutes, making sure they all get fried a little. Add the vegetables and fry on, not too fast, for 5 minutes; then add the tomato purée and stir well. Add most of the butter, cut into cubes. Stir on, and when the butter is happily absorbing the prawn and vegetable flavours add the water. Bring to the boil. Add the remaining butter and when it has melted, reduce the heat as low as possible, preferably using a heat-absorbent mat. Let it barely cook for 45–60 minutes. Then strain it into a bowl and refrigerate.

Most of the butter will set at the top. Some will remain liquid at the bottom. Remove the set butter, divide it into convenient portions, wrap them in foil and store in fridge.

Re-heat the liquid portion, and let it cook gently for 30 minutes. Strain, refrigerate and store the butter which sets second time round.

Recipes in which prawn butter makes a useful contribution include: BEURRE BLANC SAUCE; BISQUE DE CREVETTES; CREAM SAUCE; CREVETTES À LA CRÈME AU GRATIN; FISH SOUP; KEDGEREE; NANTUA SAUCE; RAGOÛT BLANC DE CREVETTES; RISOTTO; SAUCE AUX QUEUES DE CREVETTES; VELOUTÉ DE CREVETTES.

Prawn Cakes

Those who agree that the texture of prawns is as important as, if not more important than, their actual taste, will be reluctant to mess around with their texture too much by mincing, pounding or blending the meat. Fishcakes or fish balls are best made with fish like cod or salmon, where texture, though not unimportant, is secondary.

Minced prawns mixed with mashed potato, parsley, a little white sauce and/or egg yolk do, however, make fishcakes with a difference and are an option to be considered in times of glut or left-over (in so far as prawnivores know the meaning of left-over). And PRAWN CUTLETS are a very good way of treating the small, relatively cheap, warm-water prawn.

Prawn Chutney

This can be served as a side dish with curries and other Indo-Asian repasts, but also makes interesting canapés and hors d'oeuvres, or a piquant, palate-reviving savoury at the end of a rich meal. For canapés and hors d'oeuvres before non-spicy main dishes, the spice element should be milder than for curries or savouries.

Pound 8 oz cooked, peeled prawns with 4 chopped spring onions, a small knob of fresh ginger and 2–4 fresh chillies, according to how hot you like it. As you do so, slowly incorporate 2 tabs oil – coarse, non-virgin olive oil is rather good. The chutney needs to be quite thick so that it can be finished with the juice of a fresh lime and not become too runny. Include 2 tsps salt during the pounding.

Oh yes, this can all be done in a blender, but it has a more attractive texture, and is indubitably better for the soul, if prepared with pestle and mortar.

This is a chutney to be eaten fresh, preferably soon after it is made.

Prawn Cocktails

Or rather prawn platitudes? It would be self-deprivingly élitist to proscribe the prawn cocktail merely because it happens to have been Britain's most popular first course for at least a generation. Clichés are almost always based on genuine illumination, and the combination of plump prawns and shredded greenery with good, tomato-flavoured mayonnaise remains a splendid overture to meat or game, however much it is used.

The trouble starts with short cuts and economies. As George Lassalle puts it in *The Adventurous Fish Cook*, 'By international convention among restaurateurs, the tiny inhabitants of shellfish cocktails invariably come to the table covered in an insipid pale pink sauce and resting on a thick mattress of old lettuce designed to keep their numbers to a minimum.' The convention often includes salad cream, a heavy hand with the Heinz, and miserable, underprivileged prawns from the Orient which ought to be shrouded in nasi goreng.

But with real mayonnaise, decent prawns – this is where NORTH ATLANTIC peeled come into their own – tabasco and good tomato sauce or chutney (yes, tomato ketchup will do too) a prawn cocktail will always be a pleasure. With an imaginative choice of salad material (but not too much), it will be even better.

Mixing the mayonnaise with single cream or yogurt makes for a lighter cocktail. Marinating the prawns beforehand in brandy or Pernod shows that you mean business. The addition of curry flavour produces a hybrid – neither curry nor cocktail – which purists may deride, but which nevertheless tastes good if made with a decent curry paste rather than uncooked curry powder. In this case, the ketchup is best omitted but a little sweet chutney may be incorporated.

If your prawn starter is to be followed by a rich or creamy main course then there is much to be said for omitting the unctuous mayonnaise element altogether, and offering something much more astringent. Instead, spice up tomato juice as if for a Bloody Mary, but whisk good olive oil into it rather than vodka. All right, put a little vodka in, too, if no one's driving.

Home-made tomato juice delivers a more honourable version of the above: simmer 2 lb ripe TOMATOES with 1 cup white wine, a clove of garlic, a squeeze of lemon and, for extra bite, 1–2 fillets of anchovy. Season with salt, pepper and sugar. After about 30 minutes, mash any remaining lumps out of the purée, and strain it into a bowl. When it is cool, add olive oil, lemon juice, chopped basil (or dill or parsley), and sharpen with tabasco or green peppercorns, if you like. This makes an exhilarating starter.

Finally, for the occasion when neither mayonnaise nor tomato is appropriate, a well-herbed vinaigrette – 3 or 4 parts olive oil to 1 of lemon or fresh lime juice (or Seville orange juice) – is very hard to beat.

In all cases a generous helping of medium-sized, high quality prawns will help to redeem your cocktail from chain-restaurant mediocrity. Make sure the salad materials are really fresh.

Prawn Crisps
See KRUPUK.

Prawn Curry
South-east Asia and the great subcontinent itself have thousands of spicy prawn dishes for which 'curry' could serve as a generic term, albeit a vague one. There is no single, *ursprunglich* prawn curry, and the term itself is more likely to be used in England than in India. For other curry-related suggestions see INDIAN DISHES. Meanwhile, here are 1:   a simple south Indian prawn dish; 2:   a basic Anglo-Asiatic

prawn curry, suitable perhaps for parties as a substitute for coronation chicken; 3: an unusual curry variant from Aden; and 4: an interesting American adaptation.

*1:*Jhinga Jayaram
From Mallika Raj Kumar (née Jayaram)

> 2 onions, peeled and chopped
> 4–6 cloves garlic, peeled and chopped
> Oil or GHEE
> 2 tsps cayenne
> 1 tsp ground CORIANDER
> 1 tsp ground turmeric
> 1 lb ripe TOMATOES, peeled and chopped (or equivalent canned)
> ¼ pint TAMARIND water (or 2 tsps tamarind concentrate)
> 1 lb shelled prawns
> Salt

Fry the onion and garlic in oil or ghee for 5 minutes. Add the cayenne, coriander and turmeric. Fry for 3 minutes, stirring. Add the tomatoes and cook these for at least 10 minutes, until the tomato element is soft. Add the tamarind and continue cooking till the mixture is dryish and gungey. Finally, add the prawns. This curry needs a little salt; the chilli powder (cayenne) element may be increased or decreased according to taste.

2: 2 onions, peeled and chopped finely
> 1 clove garlic, peeled and chopped finely
> Vegetable oil or clarified butter
> 1½ tabs good, recently purchased commercial curry powder
> 1 tab tomato purée
> ¾ pint FISH STOCK made with or enhanced by prawn shells
> ¼ pint cream, sour cream or yogurt
> Salt
> 1 lb peeled cooked prawns
> Lemon juice

Fry the onion and garlic in vegetable oil or clarified butter over medium heat. When they are golden, add the curry powder and continue frying, not too fast, for about 7 minutes. The powder needs to cook. If you are using curry paste, this stage can be reduced to 2 minutes. Next stir in the tomato purée, then the fish stock. If you have plenty of time, let this barely simmer for 1 hour; if time presses, bubble it quickly for a few minutes before adding the cream or yogurt. Also add salt. Continue boiling/simmering until the sauce is reasonably thick. Add the prawns at the last minute, assuming they are already cooked, and lemon juice.

The quantities given will feed 4–6 people, depending on what else is being offered with the curry, but not a big party. Doubling the quantity will feed about 12, quadrupling up to 30.

3: (Quantities for 10 people)
   Olive oil
   5 onions, nicely chopped
   3 cloves garlic
   1 small tab turmeric
   1 tab cumin
   1 small tab paprika
   10 cardamom pods
   10 chillies, fresh if possible
   2 lb potatoes, peeled and cubed
   1½ lb TOMATOES, peeled and chopped
   Small tin tomato purée
   PRAWN STOCK or water
   2½ lb peeled prawns

In a large pan, and using more oil than usual, fry the onions and gar-lic until soft. Then add the turmeric, cumin, paprika, cardamom and chopped chillies. Cook on, and when the air is spicily scented add the potato cubes. Let these semi-fry for 3 minutes, stirring them occasionally. Then add the tomatoes. Continue cooking while you mix the tomato purée with three times its volume of prawn stock (or water). Add the diluted purée to the other ingredients, give them another stir, cover the pan with a close-fitting lid, and leave it to cook over a very low heat for 30 minutes while you sit in a rocking chair on the veranda with a chota-peg or sundowner.

Finally remove the lid, check that the potatoes are fully cooked and add the prawns.

4: (Quantities for one large helping)
   4 oz prawns (US shrimp) any size, uncooked or cooked, peeled
   Flour for dredging
   Clarified butter (see GHEE)
   1 or 2 cloves garlic, peeled and chopped
   Handful julienned, blanched carrots and celery

1 dsp curry paste
Dry vermouth
Scant ¼ pint concentrated chicken stock
Salt and pepper
2 tabs heavy cream

Dredge the prawns in flour. Sauté them in butter over high heat along with the garlic, carrots and celery. After barely 2 minutes, stir in the curry paste. 20 seconds later, de-glaze with dry vermouth. Add chicken stock slowly. Correct with salt and pepper. Add cream. Stir. Serve immediately.

A quick but excellent curry based on the formula used at Bridge Street Café, South Dartmouth, Massachusetts, where they can have it ready before you have finished your Barney's Joy or Nonquitt Knockdown.

Prawn Custard

Savoury custards are delicious either hot or cold. Using a mixture of white fish and prawns is cheaper than using prawns only, and just about as good.

12 oz cod or haddock, in one filleted piece if possible
12 oz unpeeled prawns
1 pint milk
3 eggs, well beaten
Salt and white pepper
3 tabs double cream

Poach the fish and the prawn shells in milk, starting from cold. Let them get up to simmering point slowly and do not let them boil. Simmer the fish until it is only just cooked – about 6 minutes – then remove it with a slatted spoon. The prawn shells may continue to simmer for a further 10 minutes before being strained out of the milk and discarded.

Let the fishy milk cool to blood temperature before adding some of it to the eggs. Whisk the milk and egg mixture, and return it to the rest of the milk, seasoning with salt and pepper. Whisk in the cream.

Flake the fish and put it, with half the prawns, into a buttered pie or soufflé dish, or into individual buttered ramekins. Pour the custard mixture over fish and prawns. Cover with greaseproof paper and bake in a cool to moderate oven, using the bain-marie technique (i.e., dish or ramekins sitting in a larger container, such as a roasting pan, with water two-thirds up their sides). The custard should set in 10–12 minutes for ramekins, 15–18 minutes for larger dishes.

Use the remaining prawns to decorate the top of the custard. If the custard is being served hot, the prawns may first be tossed in foaming butter. For cold fish custards, real or Danish caviar is an alternative garnish – with all the prawns going into the custard itself.

Custards can also be made with smoked haddock or cod – in which case they become a sort of riceless KEDGEREE.

Custards can be made considerably richer and more luxurious by using egg yolks only – say, 6 yolks instead of 3 whole eggs – and increasing the proportion of cream in relation to milk.

Prawn Cutlets

3–6 green chillies
1 tsp CORIANDER leaf
1 clove garlic, peeled
½ cup grated or desiccated coconut
1 cup cooked, peeled prawns, pounded or blended to a paste
1 tsp turmeric
1 tsp cumin seed
1 egg, beaten
Breadcrumbs

Chop chillies, coriander and garlic very finely and amalgamate them with the coconut, prawn paste, turmeric and cumin.

Form the mixture into small fishcake shapes. Dip them in egg and breadcrumbs and fry them in very hot oil or GHEE.

If using desiccated coconut, soak it in warm water for 10 minutes, then squeeze the water out.

Prawn Patia

Classic Parsee dish; a *serious* curry adapted for North Atlantic prawns.

3 dozen large prawns, unshelled
2 tabs vinegar
2 cloves garlic, peeled
6 green chillies, chopped
4 red chillies, chopped
Small bunch CORIANDER leaf
2 tsps salt

1 tsp cumin seed
1 tsp coriander seed
2 large onions, peeled and chopped
Vegetable oil
1 tsp turmeric
Brown sugar
2 tabs lemon juice
1 green mango (if obtainable)

Make ½ pint stock with the prawn heads and shells, including 1 good tab vinegar with the water.

Grind or blend the garlic, chillies and coriander leaf to a paste with 2 tsps salt and 1 tab vinegar. Separately grind the cumin and coriander seed in a mortar.

Fry the onions in oil till soft and golden. Remove them to a plate, leaving as much oil in the pan as possible. Fry the chilli paste in this oil for 3 minutes, then add the coriander and cumin seed. Fry for 1 minute more, before adding the turmeric and 1 scant tab coarse brown sugar. Stir well. Add lemon juice and the cubed green mango. Stir again. Add the fried onions and half the FISH STOCK. Simmer till the mixture begins to dry out; then add the remaining stock and the prawns. Cook for another 5 minutes at most to a moist, sticky consistency.

Prawn Paturi

A curious Indian dish in which the prawns are cooked inside a coconut, the flesh of which has previously been scored with a knife and anointed with mustard oil. Slices of green mango are included with the prawns, as is a chilli, and mustard-seed paste. The coconut is cooked for 2–3 hours in the dying embers of a fire.

Prawn Pilaff

A cup of rice absorbs two cups of liquid and feeds two people. This golden rule was given to two novice cooks in Beauchamp Place soon after rationing ended by the late, but never forgotten, Olive Zorian, and has been followed with exemplary fidelity ever since. When catering for particularly large or small appetites, use particularly small or large cups.

A pretty good prawn pilaff can be made with plain water, but it is better to use FISH STOCK made from, or including, prawn heads and shells.

1 lb unshelled prawns
4 cups fish stock or COURT BOUILLON

1 large onion, peeled and chopped finely
2 cloves garlic, peeled and chopped finely
Olive oil and butter
1 scant tab tomato purée
2 cups long grain rice
Salt and pepper
Bay leaf
Oregano
Paprika

If the prawns are uncooked, poach them in the fish stock (or water) for 5 minutes. Remove them and, as soon as they are cool enough, peel them. If using cooked prawns, peel them straight away without any poaching. Add heads and shells to fish stock or court bouillon and boil for 15 minutes. Then strain off 4 cups of stock.

In a heavy saucepan or casserole possessed of a close-fitting lid, fry the finely chopped onion and garlic in plenty of olive oil until they are soft and golden. Add tomato purée and amalgamate it with the onion, letting it cook for 2 minutes. Then add the rice, and stir it well so that every grain is touched by the oily mixture. At the same time, heat the strained PRAWN STOCK to boiling point in a separate vessel. Season the rice with salt, a little bay leaf and quite a lot of pepper and oregano.

Add exactly the right amount of boiling stock – and don't be alarmed by the explosive sizzle as it greets the rice (one of the cosiest kitchen chords once you know it). Stir once more, then turn the heat to very, very low and put the lid on the pan. Ideally you should put a steam-absorbing cloth, such as a clean tea-towel, inside the lid, taking care, however, to fold back the corners and edges over the top of the lid so that there is no risk of burning them. The pilaff now needs to cook as slowly as possible, perhaps on an asbestos mat or in a low oven. It will be ready in about 40 minutes, its granular integrity a joy to the eye.

Before serving the pilaff, stir a large knob of butter into it, and heat up the prawns in more butter (first foamed with paprika, more to enhance the colour than to spice the dish).

Heap the rice on a warm serving dish and arrange the prawns on top. Garnish the pilaff with strips of red and green pimento, if you like.

Pilaffs are best accompanied by a tomato salad and a separate green salad.

Prawn Sambal

Indonesian side dish; typical constituent of a rijstaffel.

1 onion, peeled and chopped
3 cloves garlic, peeled and chopped
¼ oz knob of ginger, peeled and grated
3 tabs peanut oil
2 or more fresh chillies, chopped
2 strips lemon rind
1 lb shelled, raw prawns
¼ pint TAMARIND water

Chop the prawns into pieces the size of large peanuts.

Fry onion, garlic and ginger in peanut oil till the onion is golden. Add chillies and lemon rind. Fry for 1 minute. Add the prawns. As soon as they acquire opacity, add the tamarind water. Simmer on low heat, adding salt and sugar, for 5 minutes.

Proprietary SAMBAL OELEK (or ulek) may be used instead of fresh chillies.

Prawn Stew

This is a Brazilian stew and should include dende (palm) oil. But it is *muito bom* with olive oil. For 6.

Olive oil
1 large onion, peeled and chopped finely
2 carrots, scraped and chopped finely
1 green pimento, seeded and chopped finely
1 red pimento, seeded and chopped finely
4 TOMATOES, peeled and chopped
Salt and pepper
1½ lb peeled prawns

Heat olive oil in a large, heavy pan and cook the onion, carrots and pimentos over moderate heat for 10 minutes without over-browning anything. Add the tomatoes, salt and pepper, and cook a further 5 minutes. Stir in the prawns and 2 tabs dende oil (or olive oil). If the prawns are fresh, cook them for 6 minutes; if already cooked 2 minutes.

Serve the stew with rice and MOLHO DE PIMENTA E LIMAO.

Prawn Stock

Heads and shells from, say, 1 lb of prawns
1 small onion (or shallot), peeled
1 carrot
1 stick celery
1 bay leaf
2 stalks parsley
¼ pint dry white wine or cider
A few peppercorns

Chop the vegetables coarsely. Throw them into a saucepan with the prawn shells, all the other ingredients, and 1 pint water. Bring to the boil and simmer, with the lid on, for 15–20 minutes.

Strain the stock before using it.

The strained stock may be reduced to half or one-third of its volume by further boiling with the lid off. This, of course, produces a stronger stock (fumet).

Prawn Syllabub

Whipped cream flavoured with lemon and alcohol but not sweetened makes a heavenly vehicle for crustaceans. Savoury syllabubs improve with keeping and should be made some hours before they are needed. They should be kept cool, but only refrigerated in hot or thundery weather.

8 oz cooked, peeled prawns
Juice of 2 lemons
Tabasco or cayenne
1 tsp mustard powder
Scant ½ pint double cream
Salt
Paprika
Cress (or mustard and cress)
3 tabs dry sherry

If time permits, marinate the prawns in lemon juice with a couple of shakes of tabasco (or a good pinch of cayenne) for 1–2 hours before use.

Mix the mustard powder with lemon juice to a thinnish paste. After 20 minutes, dilute it further with lemon juice and sherry so that it is as runny as single cream.

Whip the double cream until it is stiff. Stir in the mustard, and season lightly with salt and paprika. Drain the prawns and add them with most of the mustard and cress to the cream. Mix well, then distribute the syllabub into large individual wine glasses.

Before serving, strew each glass with a little more cress.

Thinly sliced brown bread and butter is nice with prawn syllabubs.

Prawn Tart

1 lb shortcrust pastry
2 shallots, chopped finely
Butter
4 oz mushrooms, chopped finely
¼ pint concentrated FISH STOCK or PRAWN STOCK
3 eggs
¼ pint single cream
Salt and white pepper
14 oz small, peeled prawns (or shrimps)
1 tab chopped parsley

Roll out the pastry and line a large flan dish or eight tartlet tins with it. Bake blind for 15 minutes at 375–400°F, Gas mark 5–6.

To prepare the filling: melt the shallots in butter; add the finely chopped mushrooms and cook them gently for 5 minutes; add the concentrated stock, bring it up to simmering point, then remove it from the heat.

Whisk the eggs and the cream together, and season the mixture with salt and white pepper. Stir in the mushroom and shallot mixture. Add the prawns and chopped parsley. Stir well.

Spoon the filling into the tart or tartlet cases. Bake in a hot oven – about 15 minutes for a large tart, 10 minutes for tartlets.

Prawn Vindaloo

Vindaloo is properly a concentrated, vinegary but dry dish rather than curry a few degrees hotter than 'Madras' as offered in standard ethnic restaurants. Here is Premila Lal's version.

8 dry red chillies
8 cloves garlic, peeled
¼ tsp cumin seed
Small lump of TAMARIND

1 tab turmeric
2 knobs fresh ginger
4 tabs vinegar
3 large onions, peeled and chopped
Oil or GHEE
Salt
1 lb shelled prawns
½ tsp mustard seed
1 tab chopped CORIANDER leaf

Grind or blend the chillies, garlic, cumin, tamarind, turmeric and 1 knob of ginger to a paste, moistening with a little vinegar.

Fry the onions in oil to a golden brown. Add the ground spice mixture and cook over medium heat for 5 minutes. Add the remaining knob of ginger, peeled and chopped, the rest of the vinegar and salt – also the prawns if they are uncooked. Stir well but reduce the heat to low. Cook slowly for 30 minutes, stirring occasionally as the sauce dries out and thickens. If using cooked prawns, only introduce them to the sauce when it is nearly ready.

At the end, fry the mustard seeds and coriander leaf in a separate pan, and pour them, when the seeds have popped and the leaf turned brown, on to the vindaloo.

Though normally served hot, this is quite excellent cold.

Prawns in Coconut Milk

1 lb prawns, unpeeled and if possible uncooked
Lemon or lime juice
2 cloves garlic, peeled and crushed
1 onion, peeled and chopped finely
Vegetable oil
3 TOMATOES, peeled and chopped
½ pint thick COCONUT MILK
Salt and pepper

Peel the prawns and make about ¼ pint stock with the shells and heads. Marinate the prawns for at least 30 minutes in lemon or lime juice with the garlic.

Fry the onion in oil until it is golden but not brown. Add the tomatoes and PRAWN STOCK. Simmer and stir until the three elements are mixed to a thickish purée. Mix in the coconut milk, then add the prawns, together with their marinade. Uncooked prawns will need about 5 minutes; cooked ones need merely be heated through. Season with salt and pepper. Serve with rice.

Prawns in Dark Sauce
Madhur Jaffrey's recipe and one of the best prawn curries.

1 large onion, peeled and chopped
5 cloves garlic, peeled and chopped
1 inch fresh ginger, peeled and chopped
Vegetable oil
1 inch cinnamon stick
6 cardamoms
2 bay leaves
2 tsps cumin seeds
1 tsp CORIANDER seed, ground
6 TOMATOES, peeled and chopped finely
5 tabs yogurt
½ tsp turmeric
½ tsp cayenne
¾ tsp salt
12 oz peeled prawns
¼ tsp garam masala
2 tabs CORIANDER leaf, chopped finely

Put the onion, garlic and ginger into an electric blender and whizz to a paste.

Heat vegetable oil in a large pan. Fry cinnamon, cardamom and bay leaves for a few seconds before adding the onion paste. Stir-fry for 5 minutes or until the paste turns light brown. Add cumin and coriander and fry and stir for 30 seconds. Add the tomatoes and keep on frying until the paste has a red-brown look. Add 1 tab yogurt and stir until it is incorporated into the sauce; then add another. Add all the yogurt in this way. Then stir in the turmeric and cayenne. Add ½ pint water and the salt. Bring sauce to the boil and simmer for 5 minutes. Add the prawns and let them heat through. Sprinkle garam masala over the top and mix it in.

Transfer the curry to a serving dish very soon after adding the prawns and sprinkle it with coriander leaf.

Prawns in Pernod

2 shallots, peeled and chopped finely
Butter

Salt and pepper
Paprika
1½ lb large, unshelled prawns (or langoustine tails in shell)
3 tabs Pernod
5 tabs dry white wine
½ pint concentrated FISH STOCK
Scant ½ pint cream
Fresh tarragon (or dill)

These quantities will make a starter for 6. One of the recipes for which uncooked prawns are more or less essential.

Sauté the shallot in butter seasoned with salt, pepper and paprika for 5 minutes. Add the prawns and cook them for 1½ minutes on each side. Pour off any butter which, at this stage, is pour-offable. Flare the prawns with 2 tabs Pernod or other pastis. Add the wine and the fish stock and boil fast for 3 minutes. Remove the prawns; continue boiling the stock and wine, but add the cream. Let the sauce reduce by about one-third before adding the last tablespoon of Pernod and the chopped tarragon. When the sauce is of an appealing unctuosity, pour it over the prawns (which have been kept warm).

Provençale Butter

This is the butter which is commonly used for snails and sometimes for bivalves such as mussels, cockles or clams. It is also very good with prawns: it can be spread on them before they are grilled; it can be used for frying or baking, and can be added to shellfish soups and stews.

8 oz butter
3–4 cloves garlic
3–4 tabs chopped parsley
Pepper
Lemon juice (optional)

Allow the butter to get soft and chambré. Crush the garlic into it and mash it with a fork until the combination is really homogeneous. Add the parsley and repeat the mashing process. Sharpen the parsley butter with pepper and lemon juice if the spirit moves you.

Unless it is required for immediate use, store the butter, covered, under refrigeration.

Q

Quiche aux crevettes

Quiche aux Crevettes

Since the final – baking – stage takes about half an hour in a medium oven, this is one of the dishes where it is almost impossible to limit the re-cooking of pre-cooked prawns to a few minutes; and if you bake such prawns for the requisite length of time, they will certainly become withdrawn and tough. Raw prawns are therefore more or less essential.

> 20 medium to large, uncooked prawns
> FISH STOCK or COURT BOUILLON
> 2 TOMATOES, peeled and sliced thinly
> 6 oz shortcrust pastry
> 3 eggs
> ¼ pint double cream
> Salt and pepper
> Grated parmesan cheese

Peel the prawns. Add shells and heads to ¾ pint fish stock or court bouillon and boil briskly for 15 minutes. Then strain the stock, but continue boiling until only ¼ pint is left.

Meanwhile, line an 8–9 inch quiche tin with pastry and bake it blind for 10 minutes in a medium oven.

Whisk the eggs and the cream together. Add the concentrated (and slightly cooled) PRAWN STOCK. Season with salt and pepper (having checked that the stock isn't already quite salty enough).

Arrange the prawns symmetrically on the quiche pastry. Pour in the cream and egg mixture, and decorate with the slices of tomato. Dust the top lightly with parmesan. Bake in a medium (to low) oven until set, 25–30 minutes.

R

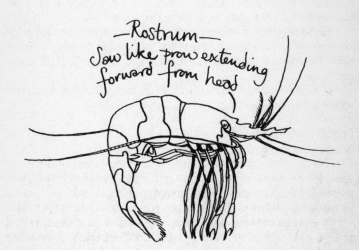

—Rostrum—
Saw like prow extending
forward from head

Rabbit or Rarebit

Toasted cheese is so delicious by itself that I always look with scepticism at recipes which complicate it by calling for eggs, milk, beer, Worcestershire sauce and, in effect, the preparation of a sauce before the grilling process. Such stratagems may make the end-product a little cheaper, but they are seldom worth the extra effort on purely gastronomic grounds. Sliced cheese (up to ½ inch thick) placed on buttered toast and grilled till brown and bubbly is very hard to beat. Piquant cheeses do not even need seasoning; mild ones benefit from salt, pepper, cayenne, perhaps mustard.

Shrimps and prawns do, however, make an attractive upgrading of this favourite instant lunch. The process is slightly more time-consuming but still impresses by its apparent casualness.

Grate the cheese; moisten it with single cream; incorporate peeled shrimps (or small prawns); spread the mixture generously on rather thick, crustless, buttered toast; sprinkle with pepper; grill till brown and bubbly.

Mild, hard cheeses such as Gruyère are better than strong ones for appreciation of the shrimps.

Ragoût Blanc de Crevettes

A luxury starter, best with fresh prawns of a good size.

Toss peeled prawns in butter. When they begin to turn pink, sprinkle them lightly with flour, shaking the pan. De-glaze with dry vermouth, then cover with double or whipping cream. Simmer very gently for 5 minutes. Before serving add a generous portion of PRAWN BUTTER.

A good ragoût-type dish can also be made with cooked, peeled prawns and white sauce such as BÉCHAMEL, especially if the white sauce has been prawnified with the crustaceans' heads and shells. Again it should be finished with prawn butter.

Ragoût de Fruits de Mer

1 large onion, peeled and chopped
2 cloves garlic, peeled and chopped
Butter
4 TOMATOES, peeled and chopped
Salt and pepper
1 tsp sugar
Thyme
1 tab flour
½ pint dry white wine or dry cider

148

16 cleaned, bearded mussels (more if you like)
8 oz unshelled prawns (more if convenient)

Fry onion and garlic in butter, using a deep-sided pan. When golden, add tomatoes (or 8 oz can), plus salt, pepper, sugar and thyme. Cook for up to 10 minutes, then shake in flour. Cook for another 3 minutes before adding white wine (already heated but not boiling). Simmer for 3 minutes, then add the mussels, and cover the pan. When the mussels open add the prawns. Serve as soon as the prawns are hot (unless you happen to be using raw prawns, in which case they should be added to the tomato and onion mixture at the same time as the mussels).

Raito
A splendid sauce for prawns fried in batter or egg and breadcrumbs, but on no account use it as a starting point for cooking raw, unshelled crustaceans (see RED WINE).

1 onion, chopped finely
2 tabs olive oil
1 tab flour
½ pint red wine and water, mixed
1 tab DASHI or BALACHAN
1 tab tomato purée
2 cloves garlic, peeled and crushed
Thyme
Bay leaf
Parsley
1 tab capers (or black olives, stoned and bisected)

Fry the onion in olive oil till it is golden. Add the flour to make a light ROUX. Gradually stir in the wine and water, providing against the possibility of lumps by making free with a wooden spoon. Add the dashi or balachan, then the tomato purée, garlic, thyme and bay leaf. Cook gently for 10–15 minutes. Then check for seasoning, remove bay leaf and add chopped parsley and capers (or black olives).

Red Wine
In general, the DECAPODA NATANTIA are sufficiently meaty to be part-nered at table by the lighter red wines as well as the more usual whites and rosés. However, they should never be cooked in red wine. A chemical reaction takes place between the wine and the chitin which produces a horrible purple scum and discolours the

whole dish. The result may not be inedible, but it certainly looks as if it is.

Rémoulade

In classical cuisine, sauce rémoulade is mayonnaise to which mustard, anchovy essence, gherkins, capers, parsley and chervil have been added.

The term is also used for a mayonnaise-type sauce which is made with hard-boiled egg yolks instead of raw yolks – or, more commonly, two hard-boiled yolks to one raw. This kind of rémoulade is more stable than ordinary mayonnaise and less likely to curdle.

Both rémoulades are beguilingly compatible with prawns and shrimp (the lobster family, too, of course).

Retromingent

An animal which urinates backward. ARISTOTLE, possibly the most distinguished all-round voyeur the world has ever known, somehow managed to observe that prawns were retromingent. And retrocopulant too. Other retromingent animals include the lion and the elephant.

Rhynchocinetes typus

The rabbitnose shrimp. Though never growing much longer than three inches, this was formerly the most important commercial prawn caught off the coasts of Chile and Peru. It was easy to catch in its shallow, coastal habitat and is much less common now, thanks presumably to over-fishing.

Rice

Rice is a better (and far more widely used) accompaniment to prawn dishes than either potatoes or pasta.

Rice Salad

One of the great stand-bys for occasions, such as fund-raising buffets, where the food should look attractive but cost as little as possible, rice salads are improved by the addition of prawns. That addition, however, may detract from the fund-raising objective.

Risotto

Risotto should be made with round-grained Italian (or Carolina) rice, never with patna, basmati or other long-grained varieties since these will not provide the creamy quality which differentiates risotto from most other rice dishes. This risotto should if possible feature MAZZANCOLLE, or some other good large specimen – 4–8 per person, according to size.

> Prawns and PRAWN STOCK
> Saffron
> 1 shallot per person (or the equivalent in onion), peeled and
>   chopped finely
> Butter
> ½ cup rice per person
> White wine
> Parmesan cheese

Use the heads and shells of the prawns with water or FISH STOCK, bay leaf, onion, celery, garlic, seasoning and a tomato element to make a handsome prawn stock. Strain it after brewing for about 20 minutes. Keep it hot and add a good pinch of saffron.

Over moderate heat, fry the shallot or onion in plenty of butter till golden and soft, at least 5 minutes. Add the rice and stir so that it begins to glisten in the butter. Add white wine – 1 small glass per cup of rice – and let it bubble down for a minute or two. Then, slightly reducing the heat, add a cup of almost simmering prawn stock. When that has been absorbed by the rice, add another cup … and another … and another. The process will take about 25 minutes, and towards the end the rice should be stirred gently to prevent it sticking. The rice, of course, will take about twice its volume of stock. When it is soft and tender (but well before it becomes glutinously amorphous) add more butter and some grated parmesan.

At this stage, toss the peeled prawns in a little foaming butter before adding them to the risotto.

Extra parmesan should be put on the table in large bowls for people to help themselves. And down with Italian restaurants where the waiters help you stingily to cheese and then take it away. (Also down with the abominable ristorante practice of grinding black pepper at your plate from a great height.)

Rock Shrimp

A major commercial species caught in the Gulf of Mexico and around Florida, so called because of its very hard, thick shell. It has an excellent lobster-like taste, but a low meat to shell ratio – about 30 per cent instead of 50 per cent or more.

Romesco

A piquant sauce or dip which goes stimulatingly with cooked prawns and other crustaceans.

Roast 3 large TOMATOES, 1 red pimento, 1 fresh red chilli and 6 unpeeled cloves garlic in a hot oven for 7–8 minutes. Remove them before they start to char. Peel them as soon as they are cool enough to handle, and grind them to a thick paste, adding salt and 1 tsp paprika. Work a little olive oil into the paste and sharpen it with lemon juice or vinegar.

Also good with fishcakes or fish and chips.

Rostrum

The saw-like prow which extends forward from the head (above the eyes) in most species of prawn. In some species it is very long, in others vestigial.

Rouille

An extremely pungent sauce in which bread (or potato) is a vehicle for garlic, a red pepper element, olive oil and often a fishy element. Rouille is meant to be very hot, but the heat comes more from garlic than chilli. Some recipes, in fact, dispense with chilli altogether and use sweet paprika instead. They have almost as much bite. Here is a general-purpose rouille, using bread.

Crumb from a small white loaf, soaked in water or milk
6 cloves garlic, peeled and crushed
2 tsps paprika
1 tsp chilli powder
1 tsp tomato purée
2 anchovy fillets
4 tabs olive oil

Squeeze as much water or milk as possible out of the bread. Put it into a large bowl and add the garlic, paprika, chilli and tomato purée. Cut the anchovy fillets as finely as you possibly can, and throw them in too. Mash all this together with a fork to make it thoroughly homogeneous. Of course this could perfectly well be done in a blender. Then work in the olive oil, spoonful by spoonful. You may decide it can take more than 4 spoons – or only 3.

If you wish to use potato instead of bread, peel and cube a large specimen, or 2 medium ones; boil them in FISH STOCK, fish soup, BOUILLABAISSE or water; and when they are easily mashable transfer them to a suitable bowl or basin. Then, using all the other ingredients, proceed as with the bread version, perhaps omitting the anchovies.

There are numerous variations and additions, and the quantities given above are by no means mandatory. Some recipes only use 2 cloves garlic; some use fresh chillies or whole pimentos; some call for mayonnaise. All are very positive.

Roux

The butter and flour base of many sauces. Oil, dripping and margarine will also form a roux when flour is cooked in them.

Melt 1 oz butter in a thick-bottomed saucepan. Add 1 oz flour and cook gently together for 2 minutes, stirring with a wooden spoon. This will produce a paste ball of butter and flour which can absorb well over 1 pt liquid.

The liquid, which may be hot but must not be boiling, should be stirred into the paste slowly at first, dissolving it to a runny consistency. Once reasonably runny (and completely lump-free), the rest may be added all at once.

If simmered, and occasionally stirred, for about 8 minutes the sauce will thicken again.

The butter and flour may be cooked together for longer at the beginning of the process, provided they are not burnt. This will make for a biscuit-coloured or brown roux, and will affect the colour of the final sauce.

In Louisiana's Creole and Cajun cooking, roux production is a lengthy, almost ritualistic process taking 30 minutes to an hour, with the roux maturing into a deep brown colour down there in the deep south.

S

Soy Sauce

essential for
chinese, Japanese
Malayan, Indonesian
and Korean Cookery

Sambal Oelek (or Ulek)

Indonesia's red pepper sauce. It is hotter and appreciably thicker than tabasco and other chilli sauces, having a granular/ketchupy consistency. Sambal oelek can be used as a substitute for fresh chillies in cooking or as a pickle when extra fire is needed at table. A useful store cupboard item which keeps well once opened.

Sauce aux Queues de Crevettes

For any simply cooked white fish, but particularly for turbot, sole, halibut, bass or brill.

Use at least 40 medium-sized prawns, raw if possible. Boil them in half a bottle of dry white wine with a bouquet garni. Remove the prawns as soon as they are cooked, and peel them as soon as they are cool enough. Return heads and shells to the wine and simmer for a further 10–15 minutes before straining the liquor.

Whisk 2 egg yolks into 2 tabs single cream. Add the strained (hot but not boiling) liquor slowly, and cook very gently in a bain-marie until the sauce thickens. Season with salt and white pepper if necessary. To finish the sauce add a small glass of champagne and whisk; then add 1 oz butter or PRAWN BUTTER and stir; finally add the prawns. (I suppose the champagne is optional.)

Sauces for Prawns

In general, the following sauces and sauce-types seem particularly compatible with prawns.

Hot or cold sauces: tomato-based sauces; cream-based sauces; sauces based on garlic, ginger and/or chillies; SOY and soy-related sauces; olive oil.

Hot sauces: BÉCHAMEL and its variants; hollandaise; BEURRE BLANC, melted butter and variants; classic fish and shellfish treatments such as Newburg, Normande, Colbert (but perhaps not Mornay); sauces based on PRAWN STOCK or FISH STOCK or COURTS BOUILLON, with or without white wine or cider.

Cold sauces: mayonnaise and its variants; ROUILLE; savoury or PRAWN BUTTERS (i.e. cold sauces for hot prawns).

Less compatible, if not actually incompatible, are: cheese sauces; red-wine sauces (particularly where prawn shells are involved); onion sauces such as soubise; fruit sauces such as gooseberry and rhubarb. I feel that mustard has more affinity with the crab family than with prawns, though fried mustard seed is essential to certain oriental prawn dishes.

Sauces with Prawns and Shrimps

DECAPODA NATANTIA make delicious and decorative sauces for most types of fish and are essential to several of the great repertory dishes such as sole dieppoise, sole joinville, sole marguéry. They do not do very much for herring or mackerel, but provide an interesting texture contrast for salmon.

There are three basic procedures.

1 Make a BÉCHAMEL SAUCE using some concentrated PRAWN STOCK as well as milk or cream, and finish it with cooked, peeled shrimps.

2 Reduce (by boiling) a generous ¼ pint dry white wine or cider to less than 1 tab. Add at least ¼ pint cream to the reduction. Finish with shrimp or PRAWN BUTTER and some peeled shrimps.

3 Make a BEURRE BLANC sauce with 4 oz butter. At the penultimate stage whisk in 2 tabs concentrated prawn stock. At the last minute add peeled shrimps or small prawns.

Scampo

Alias DUBLIN BAY PRAWN, alias *Nephrops norvegicus*, alias Norway lobster, alias LANGOUSTINE, alias karavida (in Greece), alias cigala (Spain), but in Tunisia – jarrad el bahr. With such an extensive vocabulary you can be fleeced in any currency you choose.

The true Adriatic scampo is reported to be incomparably good. This is perhaps why the Italian word for this species has achieved such wide usage. And abusage, since many another fish can be retextured and shaped into imitation scampi.

Seafood Salads

Prawns lend themselves to designer-food hors d'oeuvres, and there are endless permutations of vegetable partners – asparagus, artichokes (both kinds), curly endive, radiccio, pencil-thin French beans. Almost any salad material is suitable so long as it is fresh, though I feel that TOMATOES complement prawns better in hot dishes than in cold. In the final analysis, it is the dressing which matters most. Dressings are usually based on the vinaigrette formula (3–4 parts oil to 1 part vinegar) or mayonnaise. Here are two others which are well worth adding to your repertoire.

1 Make 1 pint really good stock with fish bones, prawn shells, white wine, onion, carrot, celery and tarragon. After 20 minutes' boiling, strain it and throw away the bits and pieces. Then reduce it by brisk boiling to ¼ pint. Cool the very concentrated fumet in larder or fridge.

Mix 2 tsps English mustard powder with 1 tab white wine vinegar (or lemon juice) in a basin. Add salt, pepper, paprika and sugar. Add ¼ pint double cream and whisk. Add the cool FISH STOCK and whisk again. Finish with fresh chopped tarragon.

2   The other dressing requires good beef or chicken stock which has been reduced to a cullis by rapid boiling.

When the cullis has set, every scrap of fat must be removed. The jelly must then be heated to melting point, at which stage 1 good tab dry sherry and a dash of vinegar (sherry vinegar if you have it) are added, plus some very finely chopped spring onion or chives. The dressing must then go back into the fridge. It can be used either in its jellied state or runny, and is particularly good with a mixture of prawns, endive and noodles.

Seafood Soups and Stews

The BOUILLABAISSE entry gives a useful method which can be adapted according to availability of raw materials. Here is a second method.

Fry onions in olive oil until golden. Add TOMATOES and garlic and simmer till tomatoes are soft. Add white wine and water or FISH STOCK, and simmer for 20–30 minutes, seasoning with salt and pepper (and compatible herbs). Strain the broth thus produced, and return it to the pan. Bring it to the boil and add rice or crushed vermicelli – 1 scant tab per person. As soon as the new ingredient is cooked, add peeled prawns (and cockles, mussels or clams, if possible).

For other soups and stews see also AYAM PETIS, BOURRIDE, Potage à la Crevette (see DUMAS ON SHRIMPS), EGGPLANT AND SHRIMP CASSEROLE, FISH SOUP, GRUNE KRABBENSUPPE, GUMBO, POTAGE AUX CREVETTES, POTAGE AUX TOMATES ET AUX QUEUES DE CREVETTES, PRAWN STEW, SHRIMP CHOWDER, SOPA DE CAMAROES, SOUTH AMERICAN STEW, VELOUTÉ SOUP and YOGURT AND PRAWN SOUP.

Shrimp Chowder

3 stalks celery, chopped finely
1 onion, peeled and chopped finely
1 small green pimento, peeled and chopped finely
2 oz butter
1 small tin TOMATOES
1½ pints chicken stock
1 bay leaf
Salt and pepper
Paprika

8 oz peeled prawns
1 small packet frozen peas

Use fresh peas and fresh tomatoes if they are available.

Cook the celery, onion and pimento in butter over low to medium heat for 10 minutes. Add the tomatoes (peeled and chopped if fresh), chicken stock and bay leaf. Season with salt, pepper and paprika. Cover the pan and simmer the soup for 20 minutes.

Finally add the prawns and the peas; simmer them for 4 minutes before serving.

To make a more substantial chowder, include some potato, peeled and cubed.

Shrimp Pie

2 lb shrimps or small prawns in their shells
½ pint white wine
Celery
Shallots
Arrowroot
Pepper
Nutmeg
1 lemon
Parsley
Puff pastry

Peel the shrimps and use the shells with equal quantities of wine and water, plus celery and shallots to make a stock. Boil the stock for at least 20 minutes, reducing it in volume from about 1 pint to ¼ pint. Towards the end, add 1 tsp arrowroot dissolved in 1 tab cold water. This will thicken the stock a little.

Meanwhile, season the shrimps with pepper and nutmeg. Marinate them in the juice of a lemon while the stock is cooking.

Strain the stock and discard the debris.

Butter a small pie dish. Add the shrimps and dot them with more butter. Sprinkle them generously with parsley. Add the shrimp stock. Cover with puff pastry and bake in a hot oven for 12–15 minutes.

Shrimp Sambol

This Sri Lankan side dish is a good disguise for the very small dried shrimps available at minimal cost from oriental shops, or for the cheapish warm-water prawns in frozen-food cabinets.

1 onion, peeled and chopped finely
2–3 fresh chillies, chopped finely
3 tabs dried shrimps
1 tsp fenugreek
½ tsp turmeric
1 tsp salt
1 tab lemon juice
1½ tabs desiccated coconut

Put the onion and chillies in a saucepan with the dried shrimps, fenugreek, turmeric, salt and lemon juice. Just cover them with water. Simmer with the lid on till onion and prawns are soft. Then remove the lid and add the desiccated coconut. Stir well. Cook with the lid off until the coconut has absorbed all the liquid.

If using frozen prawns, add them (thawed, of course) at the same time as the desiccated coconut, having cooked onion and spices in water first.

Shrimp sambol is used as a relish with other spicy food.

Sizes of Prawn
When you see prawns labelled king or jumbo on a menu or packet, you should realise that this description means middling sized to the trade. There are at least three categories which are bigger than jumbo in the US classification: extra jumbo, colossal and, wait for it, extra colossal; and there are five categories smaller than large, namely medium large, medium, small, extra small, tiny. Extra large prawns or shrimp are about twice the size of extra small, but maybe only one-third the size of extra colossal.

To keep hyperbole in its proper place, prawns are normally graded and traded, at least down to wholesale level, by their 'count', that is the number of like-sized specimens per lb or kilo. The largest, such as PENAEUS MONODON or MACROBRACHIUM ROSENBERGII, which can attain lengths of over one foot, weigh in at under 10 to the lb, under 7 even, whereas the smallest number over 700 to the lb. Apart from specialist sources, the retail range is smaller, stretching from around 20 per lb (whole, shell on) to 500 per lb (peeled, de-headed). The quality prawn most commonly available in the United Kingdom, PANDALUS BOREALIS from the North Atlantic, starts at 40 with shell on and 100 peeled (defrosted weight). As mentioned under GLAZE, packs of frozen prawns sometimes contain an undue proportion of ice. This can give them the appearance of a better count than they in fact possess. Responsible processors now label their packs with both frozen (i.e. with glaze) and unfrozen weight: 1 lb frozen weight should thaw out to give 14 oz of prawn meat.

It is worth searching out the larger prawns since the-bigger-the-better maxim applies, with reservations, to both taste and texture. The larger ones are also more expensive, of course, but usually their meat-to-shell ratio is very good, so the real price differential is less than it seems. Unfortunately, the Mediterranean countries tend jealously to guard their LANGOSTINOS, MAZZANCOLLE or CARAMOTES – and latch eagerly on to West Africa's catch; similarly, the United States has a voracious appetite for the largest American shrimp from both coasts and both continents. However, largish prawns from Indo-Pacific waters do reach our shores, often in the headless, shell-on form (frozen, of course), and these are perhaps 30 per cent cheaper than they seem since they have more meat in relation to shell. Oriental supermarkets are a likely source. Sometimes they are individually frozen, sometimes frozen in blocks of ice.

In Soho I have seen living (well, partly living) prawns flown over from Hong Kong within minutes (well, hours) of being caught. They did not look very happy or attractive, but why should they? The greyish translucence of uncooked warm-water prawns is one of the reasons the trade strongly favours cooked prawns. Given the choice, eight customers out of ten would probably plump for the eye-appealing reds and pinks of cooked crustaceans rather than the naked truth, or at least until they know better.

A word of warning: Chinese supermarkets also sell, quite cheaply, small warm-water prawns of inferior quality, suitable only for curries and the like. Sometimes the pack has a picture which indicates a much larger prawn than it, in fact, contains. So if you want large prawns, inspect the pack very carefully and do not buy anything without first verifying the size of the contents. The packaging is usually quite easy to open (and quite often is half open already).

Smoked Prawns

Prawns are not among the seafoods which have traditionally been smoked. In the search for new products, however, at least one smokehouse, Jays of Orpington, has started smoking them, and very good they are too. The ones I bought from the Army & Navy Stores, shell-on PANDALUS BOREALIS, were firm of flesh, moist and attractively smoky. They make a colourful starter in their own right or an interesting constituent of mixed hors d'oeuvres, KEDGEREE or SEAFOOD SALADS.

Sodium Bisulphite, Sodium Tripolyphosphate

These are two of the most widely used ADDITIVES or dips which are permitted in the prawn industry. The bisulphite helps to prevent the development of MELANOSIS; sodium tripolyphosphate protects prawns from moisture loss.

Sopa de camaroes

  1 onion, peeled and chopped
  2 carrots, peeled and chopped
  1 clove garlic, peeled and chopped
  Butter
  Flour
  Parsley
  1 pint white wine
  1 pint well-seasoned FISH or PRAWN STOCK
  4 egg yolks
  4 tabs single cream
  8 oz peeled prawns

If necessary make prawn stock with the prawns' heads and shells. Gently fry chopped onion, carrot and garlic in butter. After 5–6 minutes, add just enough flour to absorb the butter. Cook for a couple of minutes, then start adding the wine and the fish stock. Eradicate any lumps and simmer for 7 minutes.

Beat the egg yolks and cream together. Pour them into the soup (which has been removed from the heat). Add the parsley and the prawns. Heat the soup through gently, without letting it boil.

Soufflés

  ¾ pint BÉCHAMEL SAUCE
  Anchovy essence
  8 oz peeled prawns
  3 egg yolks
  Paprika
  Tabasco
  4 egg whites

Make a flavoursome béchamel, either using milk enhanced by anchovy essence or using milk, cream and concentrated PRAWN STOCK in roughly equal quantities.

Chop the prawns very small and mix them with the egg yolks. Season them with paprika and tabasco.

Beat the egg whites until they are stiff.

Add the prawn mixture to the béchamel sauce. Fold in the egg whites and stir well. Turn the mixture into a buttered soufflé dish. Bake in a medium to hot oven, 375°F, Gas mark 5, for 20 minutes.

Soufflé sans Sauce

Here is a soufflé calling for cream rather than the usual BÉCHAMEL – especially for occasions when God has struck again, whether for good or for His own inscrutable purposes. And if you really want to make a grand gesture of thanks or defiance, use lobster or langouste instead of prawns.

    12 oz peeled large prawns
    6 egg yolks
    1 tsp made English mustard
    1 tsp French mustard
    Cayenne
    2 tsps white wine vinegar
    1 tab concentrated PRAWN STOCK
    4 tabs whipped cream, well seasoned
    8 egg whites
    Paprika

Finely chop the prawns. Mix them with the egg yolks, mustards, cayenne, vinegar and prawn stock. Add the cream.

Beat the egg whites stiff. Fold them into the prawn and cream mixture. Stir hopefully and pour the mixture into a well-buttered soufflé dish, large enough to have plenty of room for the soufflé's expansion. This soufflé should only take about 15 minutes in a medium to hot oven (375°F, Gas mark 5), so go easy on the sherry and have everyone at table before it's ready. Sprinkle the top with paprika.

As with all soufflés, the base can be prepared in advance, but the egg whites must be whipped just before the mixture is put in the oven. Since the whites tend to absorb tastes, the base should be aggressively seasoned, unless you prefer the soufflé bland.

South American Stew

This is an exuberant but economical way of feeding the hungry.

    2 onions, chopped finely

2 cloves garlic, peeled and chopped
Vegetable oil
3 TOMATOES, skinned and chopped
2 fresh chillies, chopped
5 pints FISH STOCK
2 lb shell-on prawns, peeled (or 1 lb prawns and 1 lb fillet of cod
    or other white fish)
5 large potatoes
Oregano or marjoram
4 oz rice
12 oz peas (or small French beans)
3 corns on the cob
3 eggs
½ pint single cream
Salt and pepper
Parsley or CORIANDER leaf

Prepare 5 pints good fish stock.

Fry onions and garlic in oil until golden, then add the tomatoes and
the chillies. After 3 minutes add all the fish stock together with the
prawn shells, and 2 of the potatoes, peeled and diced, and oregano or
marjoram. Simmer for 30 minutes. When the potato has disintegrated,
strain the broth through a fine sieve, pressing the debris to extract as
much of the liquor as possible.

Re-heat the broth. Add the remaining potatoes, peeled and halved,
and the rice. Cook for 10 minutes before adding the peas or beans, and
for another 5 before adding the corn cobs, also halved. At the same
time add the prawns, if they are uncooked, and any white fish fillets
(cut in chunks). After 5 minutes, break the eggs, one by one, into the
stew, scritching them with a fork so that they coagulate in strips. Then
add the cream. Taste for seasoning and adjust.

Just before serving the stew – which is for 6 people – sprinkle
parsley or coriander leaf on top, having decanted everything into a fine
tureen, if the cooking vessel is unsuitable for the table.

Canned or frozen peas may be used, if it is not the pea season.
Canned corn would be better than no corn. If you have to use pre-
cooked prawns, introduce them to the stew at the very end, with
the cream.

Soy or Soya
Soy beans are the richest natural vegetable food known to man and, as
Tom Stobart noted in his *Cook's Encyclopaedia*, one of the dullest to eat.

Soy sauce, however, rises above its birth and is the olive oil or wine or vinegar of Far Eastern cooking. Soy sauce is a fermented product made from equal quantities of soy bean and wheat or barley, with a large amount of salt. It is essential for Chinese, Japanese, Malayan, Indonesian and Korean cooking.

Substitution

The lobster, langouste, ÉCREVISSE and SCAMPO are in the same sub-order, DECAPODA REPTANTIA, as crabs, but they eat more like their natantian cousins. Their tastes and texture are similar to prawns, whereas crabs, having for culinary purposes no tails, offer a different gastronomic experience. Even the claw meat of crabs can always be distinguished from that of lobsters. It follows that prawns can often be substituted for at least the tail meat of the lobster group and vice versa.

I am not suggesting that prawns should be passed off as lobster, only that many lobster or langouste dishes are just as good with prawns. The stumbling block is size since the tails of even small lobsters or langoustes are bigger than all but super-colossal prawns. This objection does not apply to LANGOUSTINES or écrevisses, whose armour-plated tails are no bigger or meatier than upwardly mobile prawns'. Sauces aux queues d'écrevisses are much hawked by three-star restaurants because the crayfish mystique justifies higher prices and higher mark-ups than SAUCES AUX QUEUES DE CREVETTES, but the latter are just as good.

Szechuan Prawns

1 lb headless, unshelled, uncooked prawns
3 tsps cornflour
1 egg white lightly beaten
Salt
8–10 dried red chillies
1 tab light SOY sauce
2 tsps Chinese wine or sherry
1½ tsps honey (or sugar)
1 tsp vinegar
Pepper
3 tabs oil
2 spring onions, chopped
1 tsp grated fresh ginger
2 cloves garlic, peeled and crushed

Shell and wash the prawns, de-veining them if they are, as they should be, fairly large. Put them into a marinade made with 2 tsps cornflour, the egg white, ½ tsp salt and a little water. Leave them for 30 minutes.

De-seed the chillies (which should also be rather large). Mix remaining cornflour with 2 tsps water, then add the soy, wine, honey and vinegar. Season this mixture modestly with salt and pepper. The actual cooking takes little time and the dish should be eaten as soon as it is ready, so frying should not start till other dishes, such as rice or vegetables, are ready.

Heat oil in a wok and fry the chillies for a few seconds until they are almost black. Then remove them and drain them on absorbent paper. Add prawns to wok, having removed any excess marinade, and stir-fry for 40 seconds. Add the spring onions, ginger and garlic, and continue stir-frying. After about 20 seconds, add the re-stirred cornflour and soy mixture. Stir continuously till the mixture boils and thickens. Then turn the heat right down and return the fried, roughly crumbled chillies to the wok. Mix them in and serve them as soon as possible.

T

Tempura—a Japanese
method of cooking

Tamarind

Since it keeps almost indefinitely and is indispensable for many oriental dishes, it is well worth stocking the fruit of *Tamarindus india*, a native of Africa but now grown all over the tropics. In its dried form, it is a fibrous, date-like pulp and bestows a deliciously fruity – and prawn-compatible – sourness to culinary processes. It should be wrapped in greaseproof paper or foil and stored in a tin.

The normal method of use is to prepare tamarind water: soak 1 oz knob tamarind in ½ pint boiling water and leave it to cool. Then mash the tamarind with a fork, or tease it with the fingers, and strain the water, now a fine purée, through a sieve, leaving behind the fibres and seeds. Use this tamarind water as a cooking medium/souring agent according to the recipe.

A simple tamarind sauce for fish or dry curries is made by slowly cooking 4 oz pulp in ½ pint water for 30 minutes (lid on); then strain it as above, add sugar, lemon rind and a little salt and simmer for a further 10 minutes (lid off). It is best served hot or warm.

Tamarind chutney is made by pounding or blending the de-seeded pulp with rather less than its own weight of fresh ginger (peeled and chopped) and fresh green chillies. It should be well salted, and at the last minute have mustard seed, fried until it pops, added to it, along with the frying oil or ghee.

Or you may make a pungent tamarind ketchup for the store cupboard.

1 lb tamarind pulp
1½ pints vinegar
4 oz fresh ginger, peeled and chopped
12 cloves garlic (or more), peeled
10 red chillies (or more)
4 tabs salt
8 oz sugar

Pour 1 pint hot vinegar on the tamarind and leave to soak. When cold, tease pulp with fork or fingers, and rub resulting purée through a sieve.

Blend the ginger, garlic and chillies to a paste with the tamarind purée. Add the remaining vinegar, the salt and the sugar. Simmer the ketchup for 5 minutes. Allow it to cool to hand-hot before bottling.

This ketchup can be made milder, hotter, sweeter or sourer by adjusting the relative quantities of tamarind and vinegar (for sourness), ginger, garlic, chillies (the hot elements) and of sugar.

Tamcon

A new product devised in India and now available in England, this is a sort of instant TAMARIND. It looks like a gelatinous form of Marmite, and dissolves readily in hot water, sauces, and so on. No soaking is required. Fastidious Indian cooks are happy to use it, and so am I.

Tandoori Prawns

This is a domestic adumbration of northern India's most popular process of reverse colonialism, and assumes that readers have not yet installed their own private tandoor ovens. It can be made successfully with peeled, pre-cooked prawns, though these, perhaps, are best as a first course or party nibble. For a main dish try to use large prawns, uncooked if possible (shell on, head off is a useful form). Quantities here are for 1½ lb shell-on, head-off prawns or 1 lb peeled prawns.

For the Marinade/Masala

3 tsp cumin seed
¾ pint yogurt
2 cloves garlic, peeled and crushed
Large knob fresh ginger, grated
Juice of 1 large lemon
1 tsp salt
1 tsp ground black pepper
1 tsp garam masala
Butter

'Roast' the cumin seed – that is, put it into a hot frying pan without any oil or fat and cook, shaking the pan, for about 4 minutes until the cumin aroma is pronounced and the seeds are slightly browned (but not burnt). When removed from heat, the cumin should be ground with a pestle in a mortar.

Mix together the yogurt, garlic, ginger, lemon juice, salt, pepper, cumin and garam masala, and mix them really well. Add the prawns. If they are shell-on, loosen the shell slightly, score the underside of the tails with a sharp knife longitudinally, and work some of the marinade under the shells. Marinate for 30 minutes (small, peeled prawns) or 60 minutes (or longer) for larger, shell-on prawns.

Remove the prawns with a slatted spoon, shaking them so that they are reasonably free of the yogurt mixture.

Melt butter in a large frying pan (or wok). When the butter is foaming, add the marinade. Stir-fry over medium-hot flame for a few minutes until the butter separates and the sauce at the bottom begins to thicken and go tacky. Add the prawns. Stir-fry for 2 minutes if they are peeled and cooked, 6–7 minutes if uncooked.

Traditionally these are served with nan rather than rice. As party nibbles, the small prawns should be spiked with cocktail sticks.

(There is no need to add colouring to your tandoori mix; even if you have grown accustomed to take-away magenta – the prawn shells will be quite colourful enough.)

Tango Shrimp

14 oz peeled prawns
3 tabs olive oil
3 tabs lemon juice
½ pint dry vermouth
¼ pint tomato juice
1 onion, peeled and chopped finely
1 tsp Worcestershire sauce
1 tab white wine vinegar
4 oz celery, finely chopped
2 tsp tabasco
Basil or oregano, chopped
Salt and pepper

Marinate the prawns in oil and lemon juice for 45 minutes to 1 hour.

Put all the other ingredients into a saucepan, together with 5 fl oz water, and simmer for 30–45 minutes. Drain the prawns; add them to the tango. Cook for 1 minute, and serve as a starter or side dish.

Tarator Sauce

A sort of Middle Eastern ROUILLE with nuts as well as bread; it can also include a little FISH or PRAWN STOCK, and if it does, the olive oil may be omitted.

Soak 2 slices crustless white bread in water; then squeeze out as much of the water as possible. Put the bread in a mortar with 8 oz pine nuts (or walnuts or hazelnuts or almonds). Pound them with 2 cloves of peeled garlic. Moisten with lemon juice and olive oil – and concentrated prawn stock, if you like. It must all be reduced to a smooth and creamy consistency – and can perfectly well be done in an electrical gadget providing you can face the washing up afterwards (or persuade someone else to do it).

Excellent with cold fish and crustacea of all kinds.

Tasmania

Home of the biggest écrevisses. Prize specimens can reach 2 feet in length and weigh 8–9 lb. Tasmania also boasts huge, 30 lb crabs with pincers that are 17 inches from the base of the 'hand' to the tip of the movable finger.

Telson

Sharp, pointed end to the final segment of prawns' tails. Though part of the abdomen, it constitutes the tail-fan along with the uropods. See ANATOMY.

Tempura

To occidentals the most accessible of Japanese dishes. Ideally, however, you need some kind, skilled, patient, heat-resistant person to cook the food as you and your family and guests consume it, replenishing your plates as rapidly as you empty them. The sober alternative is to cook everything beforehand, in small batches, and keep the various ingredients hot – without further cooking – in a well-judged oven.

For 4 greedy people you will need at least:

16 shelled, tail-on prawns, preferably raw
20 tiny fish, such as whitebait
12 oz fish fillets
8 spring onions
A selection of vegetables, fresh or canned, which could include any 3 or 4 (or more) of the following – broccoli or cauliflower florettes, blanched French beans, mushrooms, celery, bamboo shoots, baby corn cobs, lotus root, gingko nuts, seaweed, green pimentoes, mangetout peas
Vegetable oil for frying, plus sesame oil if possible
BATTER (Japanese)
TEMPURA SAUCE
Grated ginger
Grated horseradish
2 cups short-grained rice

Prepare the vegetables by cutting them, if necessary, into pieces not very much larger or smaller than the prawns. Keep them cool in the refrigerator until needed.

Use a clean deep fryer or wok and clean oil, the sesame element of which should be a quarter to one-third, if possible. When it comes to frying time, the oils should be hot but not smoking – 350–75°F.

Prepare the batter at the last moment, just before starting to cook.

Dip the ingredients in the batter, then fry them for about 1 minute each, until they go golden brown, in batches of about half a dozen (according to the size of the cooking vessel).

Line a dish or dishes with absorbent paper and place in a warm oven. You may wish to mix the ingredients in the dishes, or put prawns in one dish, fish fillets in another, and so on.

As soon as everything is cooked, start eating. Use the TEMPURA SAUCE for dipping, and let each person decide whether or not to add grated horseradish or ginger to his or her portion. (Each person, therefore, needs a plate or bowl for tempura and rice, plus a little bowl for sauce. The rice should be plain boiled – and slightly sticky.)

Shelled mussels and slices of crab or even lobster meat are welcome additions to the fishy element of tempura.

Tempura Sauce

¼ pint SOY sauce
¼ pint medium sherry (or mirin)
¼ pint concentrated FISH STOCK (fumet)
Grated horseradish, turnip or daikon (Japanese radish)
Grated fresh ginger

Bring soy, sherry and stock to the boil. Remove them from the heat and transfer to individual bowls. Serve the grated ingredients separately in little bowls, so that those partaking may decide which one they want.

Terrine de Crevettes

1 lb shelled, cooked prawns
2 egg whites
Salt and white pepper
8 oz salmon
Paprika
A little young spinach
A few pistachio nuts

Make a prawn mousse by blending the prawns with an egg white in a food processor. Season heartily with salt and white pepper.

Make a salmon mousse by blending the salmon with the other egg white in the same way. Rub the salmon mousse through a fine sieve. Season with salt and paprika.

Refrigerate both mixtures for at least 1 hour.

Prepare the terrine by buttering it, lining it with buttered greaseproof paper, or lining it with pork back fat, thinly cut.

Wash the spinach.

Add 1 dsp finely chopped pistachio nuts to the prawn mousse.

Put the prawn mousse in the bottom of the terrine. Cover it with a good layer of spinach leaves. Put the salmon mousse on top of the spinach. Cover with greaseproof paper and bake in a bain-marie for 1 hour in a low oven.

Tiger Prawns, Tiger Shrimp

Term used for striped prawns and particularly for PENAEUS MONODON (also known as giant tiger and black tiger). South Asian and Australian waters are a major source of tiger prawns, but the term may also be applied to the Mediterranean's PENAEUS KERATHURUS.

Tomatoes

Prawns and tomatoes are age-old allies, happier, perhaps, when co-operating in hot dishes than in cold.

Canned tomatoes and cans or tubes of tomato purée are essential store-cupboard items, particularly in the United Kingdom where, for a good deal of the year, fresh tomatoes are relatively tasteless. For all their perfection of colour and rotundity, Channel Island and supermarket tomatoes usually lack the flavour and guts of Mediterranean varieties and the bite (from August to October) of English outdoor-grown tomatoes.

When tomatoes are cheap and plentiful, it is certainly worth using fresh ones to prepare a concentrated, home-made ketchup/sauce/-chutney along these lines.

1 large onion, peeled and chopped
1 clove garlic, peeled and chopped
2–3 stalks celery, chopped
1 red pimento, chopped
3 tabs olive or sunflower oil
2–3 lb tomatoes, chopped, but not peeled or seeded
1–2 tabs vinegar
Salt and pepper
Paprika

Sugar

Fry the onion, garlic, celery and pimento gently in oil until the onion is reasonably soft. Add the tomatoes. Stir-fry briskly for 2 minutes, then add a cup of water acidulated by vinegar. Season with salt, pepper, paprika and sugar. Bring the mixture to simmering point, then clap on the lid, reduce the heat to a minimum and cook very slowly for about 1 hour. Stir very occasionally.

If the sauce is too liquid, remove the lid after about 50 minutes and raise the heat to an evaporative simmer. Stir a little more often.

When the desired consistency is achieved, strain the sauce into another pan, rubbing it through a fine sieve but leaving behind skins, seeds and undissolved bits of vegetable.

What, no herbs? Of course the sauce may be given a boost from basil, tang from thyme, oomph from oregano, or the frank finesse of fines herbes, but the thoughtful cook may prefer to prepare a neutral ketchup first and add a herby or spicey accent later.

This sauce will keep for a week or so in an airtight container in the fridge. If the vinegar content is increased it will keep longer. Even if it throws a mould on the top, the ketchup underneath the mould will still be usable as long as it retains a good bright colour. (Throw it away if it goes dark brown, purple, black or blue.)

Trasi
The Indonesian word for dried shrimp paste. See BALACHAN.

Trawling and Catching Technique
North Atlantic prawns are caught by means of a very long cone-shaped (nylon) net, which is dragged along the sea-bed a few feet above its surface. The mouth of the net is kept open by a system of spherical weights on the underside and floats on the upper side, while rigid iron wings (*hlerar*) from the port and starboard sides of the vessel keep the two edges from closing together. When the net is winched up to surface level, its exact location and length are usually delineated by hundreds of seagulls, which descend on it to select hors d'oeuvres before the main course, which soon follows. The helmsman bears hard to starboard so that the net, prawns all collected at the far end, soon forms a right angle with the stern of the trawler and can then, by strategically placed ropes, be winched alongside and the full portion hoisted aboard.

There are, of course, many variations on this basic technique: double-rig otter trawls with four bags; drift nets; seine nets (for KRILL, for example). The larger species are sometimes trapped in pots.

U

"Udang" — Indonesian and
Malaysian word for prawn

Udang
The usual word for prawn in Malaysia and Indonesia.

Udang Nenas
Soup from Surubaya (with acknowledgements to Alan Davidson, *South-East Asian Seafood*).

    1 pineapple
    Salt
    6 cloves garlic, peeled and chopped
    Vegetable oil
    4 fresh red chillies, seeded and chopped
    1 tab vinegar
    1 tab sugar
    8 oz prawns, cooked and peeled

Peel the pineapple, rub it with salt, wash it and dice it into small chunks.

Fry the garlic till golden in a little oil with the chillies. Add 1 pint water and bring to the boil. Add pineapple, vinegar, sugar, 1 tsp salt and finally the prawns. When the mixture returns to the boil it is ready.

Udang Sambal

    1 lb shelled raw prawns
    1 onion, peeled and chopped finely
    3 cloves garlic, peeled and chopped
    Scant tsp finely grated fresh ginger
    2 tabs vegetable oil
    3–4 fresh chillies, seeded and chopped (or 1 tsp SAMBAL OELEK)
    2 strips lemon peel (no pith)
    5 tabs TAMARIND water
    1 tsp sugar (palm sugar if possible)
    1 tsp salt

Chop the prawns into small pieces.

Fry onion, garlic and ginger in oil until onion is soft. Add chillies and lemon peel, then the prawns. Stir and fry until the prawns change colour. Add the tamarind water, sugar and salt, and simmer till the sauce thickens and the oil begins to separate.

A useful side dish from Indonesia. It can be made with cooked prawns so long as they are held back to the very end.

Udang Sambal Goreng

6 CURRY LEAVES
1 onion, peeled and chopped finely
2 or more fresh chillies, seeded and chopped
3 cloves garlic, peeled and chopped
2 tabs peanut oil
1 lb raw prawns
3 tabs concentrated PRAWN STOCK
¼ pint COCONUT CREAM
Salt and sugar

Fry the curry leaves, onion, chillies and garlic in the peanut oil on lowish heat for about 5 minutes. Add prawns and stir-fry until they change colour. Add stock, coconut cream and about 1 tsp each salt and sugar. Simmer until liquid thickens and the oil begins to separate.

Again this can be made with cooked prawns so long as they are only put into the coconut sauce at the last moment. (The prawn stock is optional, but, as the prawns have to be shelled anyway, the shells might as well be used. Don't worry, however, if you only have pre-shelled prawns for this dish. A little SAMBAL OELEK may be added with the coconut cream, and sambal oelek may be substituted altogether for the chillies, if fresh ones are not available.)

V

Vol au Vents

Made with Bechamel Sauce

Vandalism

Though in general a major, if involuntary boon to mankind, certain species of prawn going about their natural business vandalise crops. In Malaysia, for instance, the shrimp known as udang ketak digs large burrows, often tunnelling through the dykes which protect paddy-fields from the sea in tidal areas. The burrows let the fresh water out and salt water in, according to the state of the tide, and can spell disaster for rice crops.

A similar shrimp (*Callianassa*) can pose a threat to oyster farming by burrowing under the retaining walls of the oyster pans. This allows water to drain out of the pans and leaves young oysters exposed to the fatal heat of the sun. Sometimes it undermines the walls themselves. Moreover, the shrimps' excavations may cover the young oyster spat with silt and suffocate it (whereas older oysters can survive the silt until the next tide washes it away). From Waldo Schmitt, *Crustaceans*.

Crabs, however, seem much more dangerous and predatory than prawns.

Vein

The intestinal tract, which carries waste matter for excretion and runs from the prawn's stomach along the length of the tail. Though harmless, the vein may be considered unsightly, and is easily removed if loosened with the tip of a sharp knife and pulled away with finger and thumb. It is worth doing this with the larger prawns, but not with small ones. Where the prawns are served in their shells, deveining is impractical.

The Americans and the Japanese are very keen on deveining.

Velouté de Crevettes

Velouté sauce is made from a flour-and-butter ROUX, as is BÉCHAMEL SAUCE, except that FISH STOCK is used instead of milk (or cream). In its own right it makes a pleasantly serviceable adjunct to poached or grilled fish, so long as the fish stock is honest and flavoursome. Velouté sauce is also the starting point for rich and luscious velouté soups. For velouté de crevettes you will need:

    12 oz unshelled prawns
    2 oz mushrooms, chopped finely
    1 stalk celery, chopped finely
    2 shallots, peeled and chopped finely
    Butter
    2 tabs brandy

Large glass white wine
1½ pints velouté sauce (made with 1½ oz butter, 1½ oz
   flour, 1½ pints fish stock)
2 egg yolks
¼ pint cream
Salt and pepper
Parsley butter

Peel the prawns. Sauté the mushrooms, celery and shallots gently in butter (using quite a large pan) for 5 minutes. Add the prawn shells and heads, raise the heat a little, and fry for another 5 minutes, stirring so that all shells are exposed to heat and butter. Then flare the pan with brandy. When the flames die, add the white wine and, when the wine is simmering, add the velouté sauce. Simmer gently for 8–10 minutes, then strain out the bits and pieces.

Whisk egg yolks and cream together. Add them to the strained soup, now very hot but definitely not boiling. Stir the mixture over minimal heat until it thickens further. Taste for seasoning. Stir in about 1 oz parsley butter (or add butter and chopped parsley), and at the very end, add the prawns. (Add them sooner, of course, if they happen to be uncooked.)

Vinegar Cream Sauce
An excellent nineteenth-century English sauce for sole, turbot or cod.

1 tsp flour
3 oz butter
Salt
Powdered mace
Cayenne
½ pint single cream
1 tab white wine vinegar (or chilli vinegar)
1 tsp anchovy essence
4 oz peeled shrimps

Knead the flour into the butter. Dissolve the mixture over low heat and when melted season with salt, mace and cayenne. When beginning to foam, gradually add the cream, stirring to prevent formation of lumps. When all the cream is involved and simmering, add vinegar and anchovy essence. Finally, add peeled shrimps.

Vol-au-vents

> Scant 8 oz white fish fillet (sole for preference)
> Scant pint BÉCHAMEL SAUCE
> 4 oz mushrooms (and/or truffles), chopped
> 12 oz shelled prawns
> 6 bantams', quails' or gulls' eggs
> 6 large vol-au-vent cases

Cook the white fish in the béchamel until it disintegrates and merges with the sauce. At the same time mix the mushrooms with the prawns.

Boil the eggs so that the whites are set and the yolks are runny – 2–3 minutes, depending on size. Plunge them into ice-cold water, then peel them carefully.

Spoon a layer of the béchamel mixture into each vol-au-vent case. Put a portion of prawns and mushrooms in next. Secrete an egg among the prawns. Cover with more béchamel, and surmount with one (retained) prawn. Bake in a hot oven for 10 minutes.

W

Wok chilli Prawns

Warning Signs for Prawns, Shrimps and Crabfish

'The two first, if stale, will be limber, and cast a kind of slimy smell, their colour fading, and they slimy; the latter will be limber in their claws and joints, their red colour turn blackish and dusky, and will have an ill smell under their throats; otherwise all of them are good.' From Mrs Glasse, *The Art of Cookery Made Plain and Easy*.

White of Egg

Egg whites mixed with cornflour in the ratio of 1 white to 3 tabs flour make a good batter substitute for deep-frying and wok cooking.

White Wine Sauce

Possibly the best basic sauce for prawns, other shellfish and fish in general – and almost the simplest.

> Up to ½ pint dry white wine or dry cider
> Up to ½ pint single cream
> Salt and pepper

Boil the wine until it is reduced in volume to 1 scant tab. Stir in the cream. Season with salt and pepper. Bring to boiling point and simmer for 2–3 minutes.

That's all that is necessary, but the sauce is variable and versatile. Herbs can be added – basil, tarragon or dill will all give different but pleasing effects, as will chervil, parsley, marjoram, fennel or mixed herbs. The sauce may be sharpened with spices, for example, green peppercorns, paprika or cayenne. The wine may be reduced with shallots or fresh ginger or celery or root fennel. At the risk of painting the lily, this sauce may sometimes be finished with PRAWN BUTTER.

White Prawns, White Shrimp, Whiteleg Shrimp

Warm-water prawns and shrimp are sometimes sub-divided into two broad categories – white and brown. This is convenient for the trade, and broadly the United States prefers white while Japan appreciates brown. However, it is impossible to tell a brown prawn from a white one once it has been cooked, and the difference in taste and texture between the two is negligible, so this classification is academic as far as the cook is concerned.

Many individual species are known colloquially as white/blanc/-blanco in different regions. PENAEUS VANNAMEI (much farmed) is called whiteleg, *Penaeus setiferus* is northern white shrimp in the United States, and *Penaeus schmitti* is the southern white.

Why Prawns Go Bad Quickly

Prawns contain the amino acid glycin. Bacteria produce a chemical change in this acid if the prawns are kept for longer than two days at 55°F. A fishy smell and flavour indicates that deterioration has started.

Why Prawns Turn Red When Cooked

The hydrocarbon carotene ($C_{40}H_{56}$) is responsible for the orange or golden-yellow colours in butter, autumn leaves or, of course, the eponymous carrot. A closely related hydrocarbon, astaxanthin ($C_{40}H_{52}O_4$), which occurs in the shells of prawns and lobsters, is in fact pink or red. It looks greyish, bluish, brownish or black before the shellfish are cooked because it is wrapped in a protein. As the fish cook, the protein quickly uncoils, liberating the true colour of the astaxanthin molecule.

Astaxanthin is also responsible for the colour of salmon.

Wok Dishes

A comprehensive survey of wok-cooked prawn dishes from China and its culinary satellites would cover hundreds of pages and need years of delicious research. Yet the diversity perhaps is more apparent than real, the variations of detail marginal.

Wok-braised Prawns

6 tabs oil
4 oz spring onions, diced
½ oz fresh ginger, peeled and sliced
3 cloves garlic, peeled
16 well-grown prawns in shell, head off, raw
2 tsps sugar
Salt
2 tabs rice wine (or sherry)
2 tsps vinegar
Pepper
2 tsps cornflour
2–3 tabs tomato juice

Heat the oil in the wok and fry onions, ginger and whole garlic cloves for 2 minutes; add the prawns and fry for another 2 minutes; then add sugar, salt, rice wine, vinegar and pepper.

Amalgamate the cornflour and the tomato juice. Pour the mixture into the wok and stir-braise for 5 minutes.

Wok Chilli Prawns

16 large shelled prawns
3 tabs cornflour
1 egg white
Salt
Vegetable oil
2 cloves garlic, peeled and chopped finely
3 fresh chillies, de-seeded and chopped
1 oz fresh ginger, peeled and sliced finely
1 tsp sugar
4 tabs SOY sauce
2 tabs vinegar

If the prawns are of generous proportions, devein them and cut them lengthways along the underside so that they can be fanned out like butterflies.

Mix the cornflour with the egg white and season it with salt. Mix in the prawns and cover each with a good coating.

Heat oil in wok and fry prawns for 3–4 minutes in 2 batches unless the wok is enormous. When cooked and golden, remove them to a plate lined with absorbent paper.

Pour most of the frying oil out of the wok, leaving just enough to fry the garlic, chillies and ginger. After 1½ minutes, add the sugar, soy and vinegar. Cook for a further 2 minutes, before returning the prawns to the wok and simmering them in the sauce for 1–2 minutes.

X

Xiphopenaeus Kroyeri
PRAWNS
widely used for peeling and canning

Xiphopenaeus kroyeri

One of the most plentiful species of the American east coast – found from North Carolina to Brazil. It is known as the seabob, and although it only yields about 35 per cent meat it is widely used for peeling and canning. Seabobs are small to medium in size (up to about 5 inches).

yoghurt and prawn soup

Yogurt and Prawn Soup

1 large cucumber
Salt
1 can beef consommé
1 pint yogurt
½ pint single cream
¼ pint tomato juice (optional)
Worcestershire sauce
Tabasco
12 oz peeled, cooked prawns
Chives, chopped

Wash and grate the cucumber. Cover it with salt and leave it to drain for 15–30 minutes.

Warm the consommé sufficiently to render it liquid, then mix it with the yogurt, cream and (if used) tomato juice. Season the mixture with Worcestershire sauce and tabasco, about 1 tsp of each, but less or more according to taste. Add the cucumber and stir well.

Chop the prawns into halves, thirds or quarters according to their size. Add them to the soup, and refrigerate the whole mixture for about 1 hour.

Before serving the soup, stir in some chopped chives and sprinkle some more on top.

Z

Zarzuela

~ a Spanish Sea food dish ~

Zarzuela

This seafood operetta from Spain has a boisterous cast, a sizzling plot and a happy ending.

    2 lb mussels (in shell)
    1 lb squid
    1 lb firm-fleshed white fish
    1 lb prawns
    1 large onion, peeled and chopped finely
    3 cloves garlic, peeled and chopped finely
    Olive oil
    6 TOMATOES, peeled and chopped
    ¼ pint white wine
    1 chilli, seeded and chopped
    Saffron
    1 tsp paprika
    ¼ pint concentrated FISH STOCK
    1 tab Spanish brandy
    Black olives, de-stoned and chopped
    2–3 tabs chopped parsley

Wash and de-beard the mussels. Cook them in a little water until they open.

Prepare the other seafood, cutting squid into small pieces and the firm fish into larger pieces. The prawns may be shelled or unshelled.

Using a large pan, fry the onion and garlic, finely chopped, in olive oil. Add the tomatoes and the squid to the onion. Cook for 7–10 minutes. Add white wine, chilli, saffron, paprika and fish stock. Simmer for 5 minutes. Add the pieces of white fish and cook them gently for about 7 minutes before adding the de-shelled mussels, the prawns, a shot of brandy, a handful of black olives and the parsley.

Zoologists at Night

Nocturnal zoologists in Malaysia were charmed, on an expedition led by Lord Cranbrook, to find streams alive with what seemed to be aquatic fireflies – disembodied points of bright, orange-red light. Then they noticed that their fireflies always moved in pairs ... The explanation was simple: powerful torches were being reflected in the eyes of fresh-water prawns, young MACROBRACHIUM ROSENBERGII, whose bodies were otherwise translucent, in much the same way as cats' eyes on the road reflect car headlights.

Bibliography

Aristotle, *Generation of Animals*, trans. A.L. Peck, (Harvard University Press, Heinemann, 1963).

—, *Historia Animalum*, trans. A. L. Peck (Heinemann, Harvard University Press, 1965).

P.W. Atkins, *Molecules* (Scientific American Library, 1987).

Ursula Bourne, *Portuguese Cookery* (Penguin, 1973).

Elizabeth David, *Italian Food* (Macdonald, 1954).

Alan Davidson, *South-East Asian Seafood* (Federal Publications, Singapore, 1977).

Alan and Jane Davidson, *Dumas on Food* (Oxford University Press, 1987), recipes and anecdotes from Alexandre Dumas père, *Grande Dictionnaire de Cuisine*.

Ian Dore and Claus Frimodt, *Shrimp of the World* (Osprey Books, USA, Scandinavian Fishing Year Book, Denmark, 1987).

Alexander Filippini, *The International Cook Book* (Doubleday, Page, New York, 1907).

A.A. Fincham and P.S Rainbow, *Aspects of Decapod Crustacean Biology* (Oxford Science Publications, 1988).

C.E. Francatelli, *The Modern Cook* (Richard Bentley & Son, 1886).

Mrs Glasse, *The Art of Cookery Made Plain and Easy, a New Edition with Modern Improvements* (A. Millar, W. Law and R. Cater, London; T. Wilson and R. Spence, York, 1789).

Victor Gordon, *The English Cookbook* (Jonathan Cape, 1985).

Sheila Hutchins, *English Recipes* (Methuen, 1967).

Madhur Jaffrey, *Eastern Vegetarian Cooking* (Jonathan Cape, 1983).

Madhur Jaffrey's Indian Cookery (BBC, 1982).

Premila Lal's Indian Recipes (Faber & Faber, 1968).

E. Ray Lankester, *A Treatise on Zoology* (Adam & Charles Black, 1909).

Elizabeth Lambert Ortiz, *The Book of Latin American Cooking* (Penguin, 1985).

George Lassalle, *The Adventurous Fish Cook* (Pan, 1978).

Anna MacMiadhchàin, *Spanish Regional Cookery* (Penguin, 1976).

T. Moule, *Heraldry of Fish* (John van Voorst, London, 1842).

Narayani V. Nayak, *500 Easy Recipes* (published by the author, Secunderabad, 1965).

Pliny secundus, *Natural History*, trans. H. Rackham and W.H.S. Jones (Harvard University Press, Heinemann, 1975).

Waldo Schmitt, *Crustaceans* (University of Michigan Press, 1965).

P. Morton Shand, *A Book of Food* (Jonathan Cape, 1927).

Charmaine Solomon, *The Complete Asian Cookbook* (Summit Books, Sydney, 1979).

Constance Spry and Rosemary Hume, *The Constance Spry Cookery Book* (Dent, 1960).

Tom Stobart, *The Cook's Encyclopaedia* (Papermac, 1982).